Naturally!

Livre d'activités

Patrick Boudias, enseignant en anglais au LEGTPA Marie Durand de Nîmes-Rodilhan (30)

Robert Burbaud, inspecteur de l'enseignement agricole, langues vivantes : anglais

Kristell Corvellec, enseignante en anglais à l'ENILIA-ENSMIC de Surgères (17)

SOMMAIRE

CULTIVER, TRANSFORMER

Thème 1

Bien-être animal
p. 18

Thème 2

Biotechnologie
p. 24

Thème 3

Étude d'un produit
p. 30

Thème 4

Productions biologiques
p. 36

AMÉNAGER L'ESPACE NATUREL

Thème 5

Aménagement
de l'espace p. 44

Thème 6

Gestion de l'espace rural,
cynégétique p. 50

Thème 7

Jardins
p. 56

Thème 8

Parcs nationaux
p. 62

PROTÉGER, PROMOUVOIR LES PRATIQUES RESPECTUEUSES DE L'ENVIRONNEMENT

ANIMER, ACCUEILLIR

Avant-propos

Naturally!, Natürlich! et *¡Natural!* sont trois livres d'activités en langues vivantes, prenant exclusivement appui sur des thématiques agro-environnementales, thématiques souvent méconnues et pourtant au cœur des enjeux de nos sociétés.

Ces trois ouvrages répondent à une demande spécifique. Ils prennent plus spécialement en compte les programmes du baccalauréat professionnel (Bac Pro) de l'enseignement agricole français. Ils explorent un domaine particulier présenté dans les documents officiels d'accompagnement aux programmes linguistiques des différentes filières de ce diplôme. Ce domaine, le cinquième, qui s'ajoute à ceux définis par l'Éducation nationale, est intitulé *produire et préserver*. Il se décline en quatre grandes parties. Les trois livres, en anglais, en allemand et en espagnol, identiques sur la forme, proposent une même approche méthodologique, les mêmes thèmes et un même sommaire. Seuls les documents, authentiques, et les contenus didactiques sont différenciés selon les langues.

Naturally!, Natürlich! et *¡Natural!* proposent 16 thèmes correspondant à 16 tâches présentées pour les niveaux A2 et B1, dans une approche résolument actionnelle dans le droit fil du Cadre européen commun de référence pour les langues (CECRL). Ils s'adressent aux enseignants, mais peuvent être aussi librement utilisés par les apprenants. Chaque tâche doit être considérée comme une mission à remplir à partir du dossier documentaire, des pistes pédagogiques et des outils fournis. Les documents audio et vidéo sont disponibles sur le site compagnon de l'ouvrage.[1]

Naturally!, Natürlich! et *¡Natural!* sont une contribution à l'enseignement et à la formation professionnelle aux métiers de l'agriculture, de la forêt, de la nature et des territoires mais ont l'ambition plus générale de permettre à tous d'approcher, par les langues, les problématiques de la ruralité et de l'environnement. Complétant les manuels scolaires du collège, du lycée et de l'enseignement supérieur, ces livres d'activités permettent de découvrir autrement différentes cultures, dans leur tradition et leur modernité, de s'ouvrir à des dimensions écologiques et plus largement environnementales, qui ne négligent pas les aspects scientifiques et techniques. Ces trois ouvrages permettent aussi de travailler, dans le même temps, la même thématique dans plusieurs langues et d'enrichir aisément les connaissances en croisant les informations.

Nous formulons le souhait que cette démarche à trois voix vous soit profitable.

Les auteurs

---

1. http://editions.educagri.fr/naturally – Identifiant : naturally – Mot de passe : LA1101

Conseils pédagogiques

Enseigner la compréhension de l'oral

1. Objectif

– Permettre aux apprenants de toujours mieux comprendre ce qu'ils entendent dans des situations réelles de communication.
– Employer, à cette fin, leurs connaissances linguistiques de la langue étrangère mais aussi des stratégies d'apprentissage et de communication, qui les aident à traiter l'information de la manière la plus rapide et la plus efficace.

2. Mise en œuvre : principes généraux

Respecter la spécificité de la langue orale

La langue orale se différencie fondamentalement de la langue écrite. C'est un continuum sonore qui se caractérise par la rapidité de transmission du message et son caractère fugitif (la mémoire à court terme est d'environ vingt secondes), des redites, des hésitations, des phrases inachevées ou tronquées, une syntaxe simplifiée, voire différente, une grammaire propre. Pour toutes ces raisons, elle est beaucoup plus opaque que la langue écrite. À cela s'ajoute pour les francophones, habitués à une langue syllabique, la difficulté à comprendre une langue accentuée.

Il faut faire prendre conscience aux apprenants que la grammaire ne se réalise pas de la même façon à l'oral et à l'écrit.
Plus généralement, les règles de l'écrit ne s'appliquant pas au code oral, il est impératif de différencier l'enseignement de ces deux codes.

Entraîner à la compréhension orale

La compréhension orale est une activité exigeante qui nécessite une concentration intense ; c'est pourquoi il convient de ne pas proposer de documents trop longs : deux minutes semblent une durée à ne pas dépasser.

De même qu'il existe des modes de lecture différents suivant la nature du document écrit, on distingue plusieurs types d'écoute : globale (identifier qui parle, à quel sujet et dans quel but), sélective (rechercher ou vérifier des informations ponctuelles), détaillée ou exhaustive (découvrir tous les termes d'un énoncé). La modalité d'écoute retenue est fonction des documents utilisés et de l'objectif visé.

Le travail de compréhension orale doit être mis en œuvre de façon à favoriser l'activité des apprenants.
Tout d'abord, il est impératif que, lors de la préparation du cours, l'enseignant utilise prioritairement, comme support de travail, l'enregistrement et non le script. Il analyse alors finement les obstacles que les apprenants peuvent rencontrer et propose des stratégies pour les aider à les surmonter.

Lors de la phase de pré-écoute, trois mots sont essentiels : concentration, curiosité, contexte.
Cette phase vise à mettre les apprenants « en position d'auditeurs engagés », à susciter leur curiosité et à mobiliser leurs connaissances, qu'elles soient linguistiques ou extra-linguistiques, à les amener à émettre des hypothèses sur le document, et donc à créer les conditions d'une écoute attentive.
À cet effet, on peut s'appuyer sur un document iconographique, une vidéo, un objet, un mot-clé. Le tableau « noir » s'avère à ce moment un auxiliaire précieux : on y note les hypothèses émises par les apprenants, le lexique qu'on les amène à remobiliser, tout ce qui permet de soutenir l'activité du moment.

On peut, à ce stade, expliquer les quelques mots et expressions-clés qui constitueraient un obstacle insurmontable à la compréhension, en accordant une attention toute particulière à leur prononciation. Il ne s'agit surtout pas d'enseigner un lexique au travers de la compréhension orale.

La pré-écoute ne constituant qu'une introduction, en aucun cas elle ne doit empiéter sur le temps nécessaire à l'exposition à la langue orale.

Pendant la phase de compréhension globale, il faut entraîner l'apprenant à repérer et tirer parti des éléments extra-linguistiques (bruits, ton des voix, nombre de locuteurs, accents), à identifier le type du support (poème, discours, bulletin météorologique, etc.) et à en tirer des conclusions utiles : selon qu'il s'agit d'un bulletin météo, d'une interview ou autre, on peut s'attendre à un lexique et des structures spécifiques, un jeu de questions et de réponses, etc.

Vient ensuite le moment de la compréhension détaillée : un travail de va-et-vient entre émission d'hypothèses et vérification constitue le fondement de l'activité de compréhension orale ; cela implique des retours fréquents au document sonore, des échanges dans la classe pour confrontation et vérification. On assiste alors au passage constant d'une activité langagière à une autre : compréhension et expression orale puis écrite. Tout ce travail se fait obligatoirement en langue étrangère ; il est ponctué de brèves pauses qui visent à une mise en commun afin de s'assurer de la compréhension de tous. L'utilisation du tableau « noir » est, à ce moment, essentielle : prise en notes des contributions des apprenants, correction, enrichissement aboutissant à la rédaction d'un compte rendu organisé. Comme on n'entend bien que ce à quoi l'on s'attend, il est utile de fixer des tâches aux apprenants afin de susciter des écoutes ciblées : repérer le lieu de l'action, l'âge des personnages, etc. C'est ce que proposent les fiches d'aide à la compréhension, que l'on trouve très fréquemment dans les préparations. Ces fiches sont intéressantes car, contrairement au questionnement professoral, elles permettent à chaque apprenant d'être actif. Cependant, elles ne sont que des outils : l'enseignant doit progressivement montrer aux apprenants comment construire leurs propres outils de décodage, prendre des notes et finalement se passer des fiches.

Le cas de la vidéo (image et son)

Si l'approche globale d'un document vidéo s'appuie sur les deux composantes image et son, l'inadéquation entre les images et le message, très majoritairement contenu dans la bande-son, constitue un handicap majeur pour la compréhension orale. Si l'enseignant souhaite cependant procéder à un travail de compréhension orale détaillée, il « neutralise » l'image afin que les apprenants concentrent leur attention sur le son. Pour ce faire, il travaille, de manière habituelle, à partir de la bande-son, qui a été préalablement enregistrée sur un support audio.

Aider à la compréhension orale

L'aide à la compréhension orale est indispensable pour une compétence que les apprenants abordent avec appréhension. Au-delà du travail de segmentation de la chaîne sonore et de l'accompagnement fourni par le biais de la fiche d'aide à la compréhension, l'enseignant doit apporter une aide supplémentaire lorsque la classe ne parvient pas à décoder l'énoncé. Il faut donc, dans un premier temps, observer attentivement ce que les apprenants écrivent ou n'écrivent pas sur leur fiche et, si la répétition de l'énoncé minimal, à partir du support audio, est insuffisante, faire procéder à une réflexion sur la difficulté morphosyntaxique du message rebelle.

Pour aider les apprenants et améliorer leurs compétences en compréhension de l'oral, il faut leur faire acquérir, par un entraînement régulier et soutenu, des méthodes qui, réutilisées dans d'autres situations, leur permettront finalement d'accéder à l'autonomie.

ENSEIGNER LA COMPRÉHENSION DE L'ÉCRIT

1. Objectif

– Développer des stratégies de recherche d'informations.
– Exposer les apprenants à la langue écrite afin qu'ils améliorent leurs connaissances lexicales et morpho-syntaxiques.
– Fournir des éléments linguistiques réutilisables dans des tâches de production orale ou écrite.

2. Mise en œuvre : principes généraux

Compréhension globale d'un texte écrit

– Accompagner les apprenants dans l'exploration du paratexte (type de document, source, titre, disposition du texte, lien image-texte, mots en majuscule, etc.).
– Faire procéder à des anticipations et des hypothèses sur le contenu du document.
– Apporter une aide lexicale adaptée, en fonction de ce que l'on veut que les apprenants aient compris à la fin du travail de compréhension (tout n'a pas nécessairement à être compris).
– Proposer une lecture silencieuse à des fins d'identification du contenu global du document.
– Vérifier (infirmer ou confirmer) les anticipations et hypothèses.

Compréhension détaillée ou sélective du contenu d'un texte écrit

– Fournir une fiche d'aide à la lecture (si nécessaire).
– Aider les apprenants en faisant :
    . identifier la structure du texte ;
    . identifier les mots-clés ;
    . pratiquer l'inférence ;
    . prendre conscience du rôle des connecteurs dans la compréhension du message.

Types d'activités à proposer pour la compréhension écrite (liste non exhaustive)

– Répondre à des questions ouvertes ou fermées, en demandant des justifications si nécessaire.
– Mettre en relation (appariement) des dessins, des schémas ou des plans avec un texte.
– Compléter des tableaux (repérage factuel, classement, processus de fabrication).

Afin de soutenir l'attention des apprenants, de maintenir leur motivation et d'éviter la monotonie, les activités proposées doivent être variées.

ENSEIGNER L'EXPRESSION ORALE
(prise de parole en continu et prise de parole en interaction)

1. Objectif

Mettre les apprenants en situation de communication orale authentique, autant que faire se peut, même s'il s'agit d'un « faire semblant », afin de les aider à progresser dans la maîtrise graduelle d'une activité langagière dont l'apprentissage est complexe.
Proposer des tâches – approche actionnelle – permettant l'utilisation et la réutilisation des éléments linguistiques identifiés et sélectionnés lors du travail de compréhension (orale et écrite).

2. Mise en œuvre : principes généraux

Si l'expression orale puise ses outils linguistiques dans les deux activités langagières de réception – compréhensions orale et écrite – elle s'appuie pour l'essentiel sur le modèle de langue qu'offre la compréhension orale, d'où l'importance d'un travail soutenu de cette dernière.

Proposer un apprentissage régulier et soutenu des deux composantes de l'expression orale : prise de parole en continu/interaction.
Dans le cas de la prise de parole en continu, l'enseignant doit s'assurer de la participation des apprenants-auditeurs : notes à prendre, évaluation de la performance, etc.
Dans le cas de l'interaction, proposer fréquemment un travail en binôme, avec une réelle situation d'échange d'information (la démotivation est au maximum quand des apprenants doivent échanger des informations qu'ils connaissent déjà).
Si le travail en binômes peut poser un problème de contrôle de l'activité de certains, en tout état de cause, la quantité de langue orale produite est bien supérieure à ce qui se passe lorsque l'échange se situe dans la relation enseignant-classe, surtout si l'effectif est élevé.

Veiller à ne pas confondre expression orale et lecture (expression écrite oralisée) : pour ce faire, les apprenants sont systématiquement entraînés à la prise de notes ou à la rédaction de fiches, supports de l'expression orale.

Saisir toutes les occasions, en classe, de faire s'exprimer les apprenants

– Salutations en début ou en fin de séance.
– Résumé, par un ou des apprenants, du contenu de la séance précédente à partir d'une fiche support d'expression, établie lors d'un travail personnel.
– Correction des exercices : ce travail ne débouche sur une vraie expression orale qu'aux deux conditions suivantes :
   . les apprenants sont invités à relever des mots-clés ou énoncés tronqués, lors de la réalisation de l'exercice (bannir les phrases complètes qui invariablement conduisent à la lecture) ;
   . le questionnement pédagogique de l'enseignant doit favoriser la formulation d'énoncés.
– Gestion du temps de parole des apprenants et de l'enseignant : ce dernier doit veiller scrupuleusement à limiter sa prise de parole en classe, au profit de celle des apprenants.

Respecter la spécificité de la langue orale

– Des énoncés incomplets, tronqués permettent une communication effective, en particulier en interaction.
– L'usage de connecteurs est plus limité et le lexique moins étendu que dans la langue écrite.

Construire une progression dans l'apprentissage de l'expression orale
– Expression orale guidée :
      . exercices sur compétences linguistiques ;
      . correction des activités de compréhension écrite/orale.

– Expression orale semi-guidée (à partir d'un contenu suggéré) :
      . étoile sémantique ou marguerite ;
      . document iconographique décrit à un partenaire, au sein d'un binôme ;
      . formulation d'hypothèses ;
      . tout transfert d'information dans une approche communicative.

– Expression orale libre :
      . expression de l'opinion et expression dans un débat ;
      . présentation orale.

S'assurer que les conditions sont réunies pour une véritable expression orale
– Quelque chose à dire.
– Quelqu'un à qui le dire.
– Les outils langagiers pour le dire.
– Envie de le dire.

Enseigner les stratégies de contournement et d'évitement : un mot de vocabulaire manquant ne doit pas nécessairement bloquer la communication. Comme dans la vie courante, une périphrase, en remplacement de lexique déficient, peut permettre de se faire comprendre.

Procéder à des corrections « allégées » afin de ne pas rompre l'élan productif des apprenants qui manifestent une inhibition certaine au regard de la prise de parole, en langue étrangère, devant toute la classe.
Dans l'instant, seules seront corrigées les erreurs lexicales, phonologiques et morphosyntaxiques qui ne permettraient pas à un locuteur natif de comprendre le message. La priorité doit aller à la communication.

Dissocier expression orale et prise de notes : ces deux activités ne peuvent être conduites simultanément. L'observation montre que les apprenants faibles se cantonnent à noter ce qui est au tableau, au lieu de se concentrer sur la production d'un message oral. La prise de notes doit être différée.

ENSEIGNER L'EXPRESSION ÉCRITE

1. Objectif

Mettre les apprenants en situation de communication écrite authentique, autant que faire se peut, même s'il s'agit d'un « faire semblant », afin de les aider à progresser dans la maîtrise graduelle d'une activité langagière peu appréciée des apprenants tout en sachant que, si les textes officiels donnent la priorité à l'enseignement de l'oral, l'écrit n'en possède pas moins quelque intérêt : aide à la structuration de la pensée et fixation des apports linguistiques lors du travail d'apprentissage de la langue.

2. Mise en œuvre : principes généraux

L'expression écrite puise ses outils linguistiques principalement dans la lecture et dans l'activité langagière de compréhension écrite. Il importe donc de varier les supports de cette dernière afin d'exposer les apprenants à ses diverses formes.

Proposer un apprentissage graduel allant de l'imitation ou reproduction à la production, de la phrase simple au texte structuré.

S'assurer que les conditions sont réunies pour une expression écrite authentique
– Quelque chose à écrire.
– Quelqu'un à qui l'écrire.
– Les outils langagiers pour l'écrire.
– Envie de l'écrire.

Respecter la spécificité de la langue écrite
– Des formes répondant aux règles socioprofessionnelles.
– Une langue plus riche sur le plan lexical et morphosyntaxique, dans le respect de l'orthographe.
– Un message plus structuré et complexe aidé en cela par un usage de connecteurs plus nombreux et variés.

Construire une progression dans l'apprentissage de l'expression écrite
– Expression écrite guidée :
     . exercices sur compétences linguistiques ;
     . écriture parallèle, à partir de supports authentiques.
– Expression écrite semi-guidée (s'appuie sur l'écrit existant) :
     . réécriture avec utilisation de pronoms relatifs, de connecteurs ;
     . résumé du contenu d'une activité de compréhension.
– Expression écrite libre :
     . lettre, courriel ;
     . rédaction d'une note.

Privilégier l'enseignement « par-dessus l'épaule ». Les apprenants sont invités à travailler individuellement ou en petits groupes, ce qui permet à l'enseignant de circuler dans les rangs pour apporter une aide ciblée, soit au regard de la difficulté rencontrée momentanément par un apprenant, soit au regard des difficultés plus générales de tel autre apprenant. En tout état de cause, la rédaction finale est individuelle.

Donner la priorité à la communication et non à la correction des erreurs : si le travail d'expression écrite est un moment privilégié pour s'intéresser à la morphosyntaxe, l'activité ne doit pas être perçue comme un travail de correction systématique des erreurs. Ce travail de correction – sur les erreurs récurrentes les plus fréquentes – se situe en aval de l'enseignement de l'expression écrite. Il peut s'effectuer soit de manière collective, soit de manière individuelle.

Varier les exercices de production écrite en puisant dans les nombreux types d'écriture
– Écriture personnelle : courriel, liste de tâches à accomplir, journal intime, etc.
– Écriture professionnelle : compte rendu, note, etc.
– Écriture publique : imprimé, lettre de réclamation, etc.
– Écriture sociale : invitation, lettre de remerciement, etc.
– Écriture créative : poème, conte, etc.

Du bon usage des pictogrammes

Le livre est découpé en quatre domaines, chacun comportant quatre thèmes. Le contenu pédagogique de chaque thème, comme vous pourrez le découvrir à la lecture, se compose de trois parties.
En début de chaque thème, une double page présente la tâche à réaliser par les apprenants et les objectifs poursuivis.
Les trois pages qui suivent contiennent les documents authentiques qui sont le support de l'apprentissage que l'enseignant va mettre en œuvre en s'appuyant sur les pistes pédagogiques et l'énoncé de la réalisation de la tâche finale, qu'il trouve dans la dernière page de chaque thème.

Sur le site compagnon de *Naturally!*, l'enseignant et l'apprenant trouvent des documents authentiques de plusieurs natures. Il s'agit de textes, de documents iconographiques, tels que des photographies, *cartoons*, graphiques, schémas, ou encore de documents audio et de documents vidéo.
Afin de permettre un repérage plus aisé lors de la préparation de l'exploitation des différents documents, le choix a été fait d'indiquer la nature des documents, disponibles sur ce site compagnon, par un pictogramme présent dans l'encadré de chaque document.

 Ce pictogramme indique que ce document se trouve également sur le **site compagnon** de l'ouvrage *Naturally!*

 Ce casque vous indique qu'un **document audio** est disponible en ligne. En fonction des thèmes et de l'exploitation pédagogique envisagée, cet enregistrement sonore peut être découpé selon la didactisation prévue dans les pistes pédagogiques. S'il est proposé dans son intégralité, l'enseignant a le choix de son utilisation et peut déterminer lui-même le passage le plus à même de convenir à l'étude en classe.

 Ce pictogramme est associé à une **vidéo** qui, comme pour les documents audio, vous est proposée soit déjà préparée pour une utilisation pédagogique, soit dans son intégralité. Vous trouvez une présentation de l'usage possible de cette vidéo dans les pistes pédagogiques, en fin de chaque thème.

 Ceci vous indique que vous trouverez en ligne un **document « texte »** non interactif, qui constitue le document authentique ou qui est complémentaire du document authentique présent dans l'ouvrage. Il peut s'agir d'un script attaché à un document audio, d'un article complet, d'un document iconographique proposé à l'étude (photographie, *cartoon*, affiche, graphique). Il est également possible de trouver des supports pédagogiques, tels que décrits dans le paragraphe suivant.

Vous trouvez dans les pistes pédagogiques la mention de documents *bis* ou *ter*. Ces documents sont des supports pédagogiques supplémentaires, qui peuvent être des fiches d'aide, des grilles de compréhension et d'étude, ou d'observation et d'évaluation, associées à un document précis, et qui peuvent être accompagnées de corrigés destinés à l'enseignant et à l'apprenant. Il appartient à l'enseignant de déterminer l'usage qu'il en fera en classe.

Rappel : vous trouvez l'adresse URL du site compagnon p. 6.

Tableau

récapitulatif

TÂCHE	NIVEAU	DOCUMENTS SUR LE LIVRE	DOCUMENTS SUR LE SITE
Renseigner et conseiller oralement	B1	Doc.1, doc. 2, doc. 3, doc. 4, doc. 6, doc. 7, doc. 8, doc. 9	Doc. 1 photo et dessin humoristique, doc. 5 audio, vidéo et script, doc. 6 couverture, doc. 10 audio et script
Débattre sur un sujet de société	B1	Doc.1, doc. 2, doc. 3, doc. 4, doc. 5, doc. 6, doc. 8, doc. 9	Doc. 1 dessin humoristique, doc. 2 dessin humoristique, doc. 7 audio et script, doc. 10 audio et script, doc. 10bis fiche de compréhension, doc. 10ter corrigé
Rendre compte d'une expérience professionnelle	A2/B1	Doc.1, doc. 2, doc. 3, doc. 4, doc. 5, doc. 7, doc. 8, doc. 9, doc. 10, doc. 12	Doc. 6 audio et script, doc. 6bis fiche de compréhension, doc. 6ter corrigé, doc. 8 graphiques, doc. 11 audio et script
Convaincre un auditoire	B1+	Doc.1, doc. 2, doc. 3, doc. 4, doc. 5, doc. 7, doc. 8, doc. 10	Doc. 1 photo, doc. 6 audio et script, doc. 9 audio et script, doc 9bis fiche d'aide à la compréhension, doc. 9ter corrigé, doc 10 dessin humoristique, doc. 11 vidéo
Rédiger un tract	A2	Doc.1, doc. 2, doc. 3, doc. 4, doc. 6, doc. 8, doc. 9, doc. 10	Doc.1 photo, doc. 5 audio et script, doc. 7 audio et script, doc. 11 vidéo
Organiser un débat	B1	Doc.1, doc. 2, doc. 3, doc. 4, doc. 5, doc. 6, doc. 7, doc. 8, doc. 9, doc. 10, doc. 11, doc. 12	Doc. 1 photo, doc. 9 dessin humoristique
Conseiller des clients	B1+	Doc.1, doc. 2, doc. 3, doc. 4, doc. 7, doc. 9, doc. 11, doc. 12	Doc.1 dessin humoristique, doc. 2 dessin humoristique, doc. 5 audio et script, doc. 6 audio et script, doc. 8 vidéo, doc. 10 audio et script, doc. 13 audio et script
Réaliser un panneau ou une affiche	A2	Doc.1, doc. 2, doc. 4, doc. 5, doc. 6, doc. 7, doc. 8, doc. 9, doc. 10	Doc.1 dessin humoristique, doc. 3 audio et script, doc. 4 photos, doc. 5 photos, doc. 11 vidéo
Rédiger un message électronique	A2	Doc.1, doc. 2, doc. 3, doc. 5, doc. 6, doc. 7, doc. 8, doc. 11	Doc.1 dessin humoristique, doc. 3 affiche, doc. 4 audio, script et vidéo, doc. 5 affiche, doc. 9 audio, script et vidéo, doc. 10 audio et script
Réaliser une enquête et en rendre compte	A2+	Doc.1, doc. 2, doc. 3, doc. 4, doc. 5, doc. 6, doc. 8, doc. 9, doc. 10	Doc.1 dessin humoristique, doc. 7 audio et script, doc. 11 dessin humoristique, doc. 12 audio et script, doc. 13 audio et script
Réaliser une affiche	B1	Doc.1, doc. 2, doc. 4, doc. 5, doc. 6, doc. 8, doc. 9, doc. 10, doc. 12, doc. 13	Doc. 2 graphique, doc. 3 audio, script et vidéo, doc. 4 photo, doc. 5 audio et script, doc. 7 audio et script, doc. 9 photo, doc. 11 audio et script
Présenter un projet	B1	Doc.1, doc. 2, doc. 3, doc. 4, doc. 5, doc. 7, doc. 8, doc. 9, doc. 10, doc. 11	Doc. 1 dessin humoristique, doc. 5 photo, doc. 6 audio et script, doc. 12 vidéo
Réaliser une brochure, la présenter oralement puis répondre à des questions	B1	Doc.1, doc. 2, doc. 3, doc. 4, doc. 5, doc. 6, doc. 7, doc. 8, doc. 10	Doc. 1 photo, doc. 2 dessin humoristique, doc. 4 graphique, doc. 9 audio et script
Réaliser un sondage ou une interview	B1	Doc.1, doc. 2, doc. 3, doc. 4, doc. 5, doc. 7, doc. 8, doc. 9, doc. 10	Doc. 1 photo, doc. 2bis fiche d'aide à la compréhension, doc. 2ter corrigé, doc. 6 vidéo, audio et script, doc. 7 dessin humoristique
Rédiger une affichette	A2+	Doc.1, doc. 2, doc. 3, doc. 4, doc. 6, doc. 7, doc. 8, doc. 9	Doc. 1 photos, doc. 5 audio et script, doc. 10 audio et script, doc. 10bis fiche d'aide à la compréhension, doc. 10ter corrigé, doc. 11 vidéo
Réaliser une affiche ou un dépliant publicitaire	A2	Doc. 1, doc. 2, doc. 3, doc. 6, doc. 7, doc. 9, doc. 10	Doc. 1 couverture, doc. 3 dessin humoristique, doc. 4 audio et script, doc. 5 audio et script, doc. 8 audio et script, doc. 10 affiche

CULTIVER, TRANSFORMER

PRODUCTIONS VÉGÉTALE ET ANIMALE, TRANSFORMATION DES PRODUITS AGRICOLES...

BIEN-ÊTRE ANIMAL

TÂCHE FINALE

Employé(e) pour l'été dans une association de défense des animaux, vous renseignez un étranger sur les différentes structures permettant d'adopter un animal et vous lui donnez des conseils sur la meilleure façon de s'en occuper.

ACTIVITÉ LANGAGIÈRE

Expression orale en continu et en interaction

NIVEAU VISÉ

B1

CAPACITÉS À METTRE EN ŒUVRE

⚙ Donner un renseignement.

⚙ Expliquer les avantages et les inconvénients d'une solution.

⚙ Développer un point de vue.

⚙ Donner des descriptions, explications sur des lieux, des faits…

⚙ Expliquer des actions à réaliser.

Man's best friend...

 BOÎTE À OUTILS

Suggérer/ mettre en garde/ faire faire	L'expression de la suggestion	Why don't you go to an animal shelter? Please, join the fight to protect animals.
	Modaux	You must go there and see it for yourself.
		You should go to the vet.
	L'impératif et l'expression de l'obligation	Don't allow your dog in your bedroom or on the sofa.
		Take him for a walk as often as you can.
		You need to show him where he will find food and water.
Conseiller	La modalisation	I would advise you to go to a pet shop. You'd better take this dog to the vet.
Démontrer/ justifier/ persuader	Relations logiques (cause, conséquence, but)	Reputable breeders put the welfare of their dogs first. Consequently, they don't breed more animals than they can place.
		This dog looks sad because he's been ill-treated.
Émettre des hypothèses	Propositions en **if**	If a breeder doesn't ask you a lot of questions, you're probably in the wrong place.

1

Puppy mills

Origin: © Dan Phelps, www.danielphelps.ca

Origin: © Animal Folks MN/cc by-sa A. Richards

2

What is a puppy mill?

A puppy mill is a large-scale commercial dog breeding operation where profit is given priority over the well-being of the dogs. Unlike responsible breeders, who place the utmost importance on producing the healthiest puppies possible, breeding at puppy mills is performed without consideration of genetic quality. This results in generations of dogs with unchecked hereditary defects.

Puppy mill puppies are typically sold to pet shops – usually through a broker, or middleman – and marketed as young as eight weeks of age. The lineage records of puppy mill dogs are often falsified.

Origin: © 2010. The American Society for the Prevention of Cruelty to Animals (ASPCA). All Rights Reserved

3

When and why did puppy mills begin?

Puppy mills began sprouting up after World War II. In response to widespread crop failures in the Midwest, the United States Department of Agriculture began promoting purebred puppies as a fool-proof "cash" crop. It is easy to see why this might have appealed to farmers facing hard times – breeding dogs does not require the intense physical labor that it takes to produce edible crops, nor are dogs as vulnerable to unfavorable weather. [...] Pet stores, large and small, boomed with the increasing supply of puppies from the new "mills". Today, Missouri is considered the largest puppy mill state in the country.

Origin: © 2010. The American Society for the Prevention of Cruelty to Animals (ASPCA). All Rights Reserved

4

Prisonners of greed

Hundreds of thousands of dogs suffer in puppy mills in this country. The dogs are prisoners of greed. They are locked in small cages. They freeze in the winter and swelter in the summer. The dogs never get out of their prisons. They are bred over and over again until they die. The only way to free them from the misery of these horrid puppymills is to eliminate the demand for puppies by refusing to buy a puppy in a pet store and boycotting those pet stores that sell puppies. When people stop buying puppies in pet stores, the puppy mills will go out of business and the misery will end. The state and federal governments do not enforce the laws to protect the dogs. The commercial breeders and brokers have huge well-funded lobbying efforts. Please join this fight to free the prisonners of greed. The only person who is going to make a difference for the dogs suffering in puppy mills is you. You, the people, can free them from their puppy mill prisons.

Adapted from: Coalition Against Misery, www.prisonnersofgreed.org

5

Pet store puppies come from puppy mills

6

Ethical dog breeder

FOR BREEDERS & PUPPY BUYERS WHO CARE

ETHICAL DOG BREEDER MAGAZINE

LITTERS: HOW MANY IS TOO MANY?

12 HEALTH TIPS EVERY BUYER SHOULD KNOW!

GENETICS MASTERCLASS:

POPULAR SIRE SYNDROME:

Origin: © K9 Magazine

7

Finding a reputable breeder

You've decided not to purchase a dog from a pet store. [...] You want to find a reputable breeder. But how?

First, visit several breeders. Focus on those who have the puppy's parents [...] on the premises. If the parents are happy, friendly dogs, and they neither back away nor jump in your face, you're on the right track.

Check the facilities and surroundings for cleanliness and make sure all the animals are well cared for. [...]

Ask the breeder about specific characteristics of the breed and whether he or she has encountered any genetic problems in the bloodlines. [...] A reputable breeder will reveal inherited problems and discuss what he or she is doing to try to eliminate them.

An above-board breeder will also explain the quality and cost differences between show and pet-quality puppies. [...] Reputable breeders put the welfare of their dogs first. Consequently, they don't breed more animals than they can place and their main concern is that the animal be able to lead a long, happy and healthy life. So if a breeder doesn't grill you with a lot of tough questions about your expectations and ability to care for a dog, you're probably in the wrong place.

Origin: © Yankee Golden Retriever Rescue

8

Dog Forum

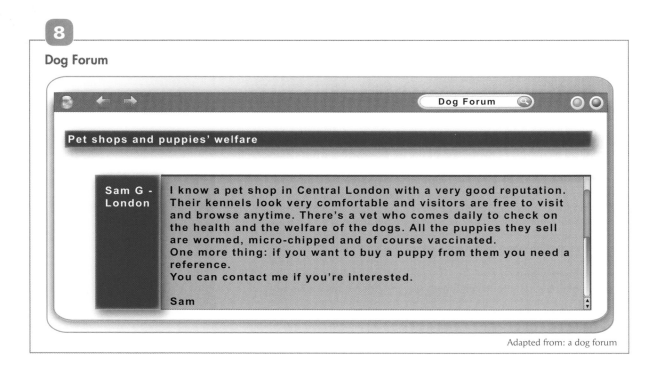

Dog Forum

Pet shops and puppies' welfare

Sam G - London

I know a pet shop in Central London with a very good reputation. Their kennels look very comfortable and visitors are free to visit and browse anytime. There's a vet who comes daily to check on the health and the welfare of the dogs. All the puppies they sell are wormed, micro-chipped and of course vaccinated.
One more thing: if you want to buy a puppy from them you need a reference.
You can contact me if you're interested.

Sam

Adapted from: a dog forum

9

Welcoming a new puppy into your home

When your new puppy first comes into a house, he needs to learn that this is his new space. Put him on a leash and walk him through the whole house. This is a time to show him everything, but also use the leash to limit access to areas you don't want him getting [...]. You should not say "no". Since the puppy has not learned his name yet, he may start to think that it is what you are calling him. Instead, let him know your displeasure by using a low voice [...] while doing a mild tug on the leash every time he sniffs something he is not supposed to touch. [...] It is important to let him sniff the item for a second before growling [...]. Dogs remember things by what they smell like, not what they look like. [...]

Now it's time to show your dog important things such as where he will find food and water, his crate, where you want him to go to the bathroom outside. The way to do this is to take him to the spot and stand there until he goes. Once he does, praise him for it. Then you can offer a tour of the rest of the yard. [...]

Note: if it took more than an hour to get your pup home from where you bought him, you should do the yard tour first so he can go to the bathroom.

By J. Saeman
19 July 2007

Origin: cc by-nd J. Saeman

10

Enforcing rules and boundaries for new dogs

PISTES PÉDAGOGIQUES

doc. 1   Ce dessin et cette photographie ont pour objectif d'introduire le sujet du thème et d'effectuer un travail de préparation à la lecture des documents 2, 3 et 4 qui traitent des usines à chiots.

doc. 2, 3, 4   Ces trois textes sont l'occasion pour les apprenants d'être sensibilisés au problème des *puppy mills*. Leur exploitation permet de mettre en place le lexique approprié et de relever les informations qui doivent être réutilisées lors de la réalisation de la tâche finale. La densité lexicale des documents nécessite une aide soutenue de la part de l'enseignant.

doc. 5   Cet enregistrement sonore vient en complément des documents 2, 3 et 4. Il a pour but de fixer le lexique présenté précédemment mais également d'introduire des outils linguistiques adaptés à la tâche finale (propositions en *if*). La version vidéo intégrale de ce document est également disponible en ligne.

doc. 6, 7, 8   Cet ensemble apporte un autre éclairage sur l'élevage et la vente de chiens de compagnie. Le document 6 a pour fonction d'anticiper la lecture des documents 7 et 8. Le titre de la publication se prête à l'émission d'hypothèses sur ce qu'est un bon éleveur de chien. Les documents 7 et 8 permettent de vérifier les suppositions faites lors de l'étape précédente mais également d'enrichir le champ lexical relatif au thème étudié. De nouveaux outils linguistiques comme l'emploi de l'impératif et des articulations du discours peuvent être mis en avant. L'étude de ces documents peut donner lieu à un entraînement à la reformulation des informations pertinentes par le biais notamment d'un tableau à double entrée : *Dog breeders who care ; Dog breeders who don't care*.
Ce travail peut être réalisé en binômes avec restitution orale devant la classe.

doc. 9, 10   Ces deux documents doivent permettre de recueillir les éléments nécessaires à la réalisation de la deuxième partie de la tâche finale. Ils sont l'occasion de manipuler une nouvelle fois l'expression de l'obligation et de s'approprier l'expression de la suggestion. La rapidité du débit du document sonore requiert l'utilisation d'une fiche d'aide à la compréhension conçue par l'enseignant.

TÂCHE FINALE

À l'issue de l'étude de ces différents documents, les apprenants doivent être en mesure de mener une conversation au cours de laquelle deux représentants d'une association de protection des animaux donnent des conseils à un étranger désireux d'adopter un animal de compagnie. Les conseils prodigués portent sur deux aspects : les structures permettant d'adopter un animal de compagnie, ainsi que la conduite à adopter lors de l'acquisition d'un chien.
Les deux représentants de l'association se répartissent équitablement les informations à dispenser. L'apprenant qui tient le rôle de l'étranger se contente simplement de poser les questions qui servent à amorcer la conversation. La durée de l'échange ne doit pas excéder cinq minutes.

BIOTECHNOLOGIE

TÂCHE FINALE

Dans le cadre de la journée mondiale de la recherche scientifique, votre lycée, en partenariat avec d'autres établissements européens, organise un débat contradictoire sur la place des OGM dans notre société et leur impact sur l'environnement.

ACTIVITÉ LANGAGIÈRE

Expression orale en interaction

NIVEAU VISÉ

B1

CAPACITÉS À METTRE EN ŒUVRE

⚙ Partager ses idées, sentiments, émotions…

⚙ Exprimer ou répondre à un accord, un désaccord, une acceptation, un refus.

⚙ Réagir à des objections.

⚙ Demander ou fournir une confirmation, un éclaircissement.

⚙ Reformuler pour clarifier ou récapituler des échanges.

To GM or not to GM...

 BOÎTE À OUTILS

Répondre	L'affirmation et la négation	I agree (with you) / I don't agree / I can't agree (with you). You're (absolutely) right! / You're (totally) wrong!… That's quite true / I'm not sure about that…
Maintenir/ relancer le dialogue	Gap fillers Echoed questions	Well / Err / Hum / I mean / Well, you see… / How shall I put it… Oh, really? How's that?
Donner son point de vue	L'expression de la subjectivité	To my mind / In my view / It seems to me that / What I think is / On the one hand I think… but on the other…
Comparer	Comparatifs et superlatifs	This plant is more resistant to diseases… It's healthier… That's the best / the worst news we've heard for a long time.
Démontrer/ justifier	Articulations du discours	Because / But / For that reason / So / The reason is / The thing is / So that / In order to / Therefore… Monsanto produces GM seeds in order to feed the world population.
	Relations logiques (cause, conséquence, but)	Thanks to, because of, since… Thanks to scientific research we can…
	L'expression de l'atténuation	However / But / Nevertheless.

1 What a huge rooster!

Origin: © AhaJokes.com 2005

2 Genetic engineering

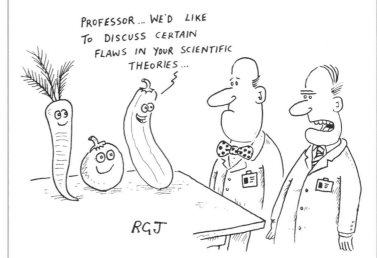

"Thats it. We've taken this genetic engineering too far"

Origin: © Jolley, www.CartoonStock.com

3 Where did biotechnology begin?

Certain practices that we would now classify as applications of biotechnology have been in use since man's earliest days. Nearly 10,000 years ago, our ancestors were producing wine, beer, and bread by using fermentation. [...]

Discovery of the fermentation process allowed early peoples to produce foods by allowing live organisms to act on other ingredients. But our ancestors also found that they could increase the yield and improve the taste of crops by selecting seeds from particularly desirable plants. [...] Plants that, for example, gave the highest yield, stayed the healthiest during periods of drought or disease, or were easiest to harvest tended to produce future generations with these same characteristics. Once the genetic basis of heredity was understood, the benefits of cross-breeding, or hybridization, became apparent: plants with different desirable traits could be used to cultivate a later generation that combined these characteristics.

An understanding of the scientific principles behind fermentation and crop improvement practices has come only in the last hundred years. But the early, crude techniques, even without the benefit of sophisticated laboratories and automated equipment, were a true practice of biotechnology guiding natural processes to improve man's physical and economic well-being.

Origin: © 1994-2009 by Access Excellence @ the National Health Museum

4

DNA

Deoxyribonucleic acid (DNA)

The discovery of the structure of DNA by Watson and Crick was the beginning of an exciting new level of understanding of how living things work. [...]

The use of living things to make useful products began centuries ago and is called "biotechnology". The discovery of the DNA structure in 1953 led to an explosion of research and the development of modern biotechnology.

Modern biotechnology is making exciting applications possible in agriculture, environment, food technology, forestry, industry and medicine. These include:

– producing human insulin for diabetics;
– using genetic fingerprints and forensic technics to solve crimes;
– bioremediation : using micro-organisms to remove poisonous pollutants from soil and water;
– biomining : extracting metals using microbes and plants;
– developing Genetically Modified (GM) crops and cloning [...];
– producing healthy tissues to replace damaged ones.

Origin: Text supplied by the South African Public Understanding of Biotechnology Programme, which is managed by the South African Agency for Science and Technology Advancement on behalf of the National Department of Science and Technology

5

Conventional breeding versus GM crops

For thousands of years farmers have used a process of selection and cross breeding to continually improve the quality of crops. Even in nature, plants and animals selectively breed, thus ensuring the optimum gene pool for future generations. Traditional breeding methods are slow, requiring intensive labor: while trying to get a desirable trait in a bred species, undesirable traits will appear and breeders must continue the process over and over again until all the undesirables are bred out.

In contrast, organisms acquire one specific gene or a few genes together through genetic modification, without other traits included and within a single generation. However, this technology too is inherently unpredictable and some scientists believe it can produce potentially dangerous results unless better testing methods are developed.

[...]

Proponents of GM crops claim that advantages may be many, such as:

– improved storage and nutritional quality;
– pest and disease resistance;
– selective herbicide tolerance;
– tolerance of water, temperature and saline extremes;
– improved animal welfare;
– higher yields and quality.

However, until further studies can show that GM foods and crops do not pose serious threats to human health or the world's ecosystems, the debate over their release will continue.

By K. Sakko
May 2002

Origin: © Sakko and © 2000-2010 American Institute of Biological Sciences

6

The green revolution

I have devoted my life to the global challenge of providing adequate food production for a growing world population. Forty years ago, a Green Revolution was started using improved seed and fertilizer, helping dramatically increase the harvest while sparing forest and natural areas from the plow. It took both the scientific advances and the changes in economic policies by leaders to allow for the adoption of the Green Revolution technologies by millions of hungry farmers.

Over the past decade, we have been witnessing the success of plant biotechnology. This technology is helping farmers throughout the world produce higher yield, while reducing pesticide use and soil erosion. The benefits and safety of biotechnology has been proven over the past decade in countries with more than half of the world's population. What we need is courage by the leaders of those countries where farmers still have no choice but to use older and less effective methods. The Green Revolution and now plant biotechnology are helping meet the growing demand for food production, while preserving our environment for future generations.

By Dr. N. Borlaug

Origin: © 2005-09 Monsanto Company

7

GM plants that use less fertilizers

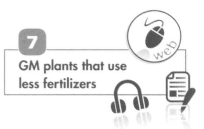

8

GE agriculture and genetic pollution

The introduction of genetically engineered (GE) organisms into the complex ecosystems of our environment is a dangerous global experiment with nature and evolution.

MONSTERANTO
HATCH ONE TODAY

Genetic scientists are altering life itself. The products of genetic engineering are living organisms that could never have evolved naturally and do not have a natural habitat.

These human-made organisms can reproduce and interbreed with natural organisms, thereby spreading to new environments and future generations in an unpredictable and uncontrollable way. Because we know so little about how these novel organisms will act in the environment, and because these living organisms can multiply and spread, the potentially harmful effects of GE organisms may only be discovered when it is too late.

For these reasons, GE organisms (or GMOs – genetically modified organisms) must not be released into the environment. They pose unacceptable risks to ecosystems, and threaten biodiversity, wildlife and sustainable forms of agriculture.

Origin: © Greenpeace International, www.greenpeace.org

9

Are GM crops killing bees?

Mysterious events in recent months have suddenly made Einstein's apocalyptic vision seem all the more topical. For unknown reasons, bee populations throughout Germany are disappearing — something that is so far only harming beekeepers. But the situation is different in the United States, where bees are dying in such dramatic numbers that the economic consequences could soon be dire. No one knows what is causing the bees to perish, but some experts believe that the large-scale use of genetically modified plants in the US could be a factor.

By G. Latsch
March 22nd, 2007

Origin: © http://www.spiegel.de/international/
world/0,1518,473166,00.html

10

Effects of genetically modified food

PISTES PÉDAGOGIQUES

doc. 1, 2 Ces deux dessins humoristiques permettent d'introduire la thématique des biotechnologies et de mieux connaître les représentations qu'en ont les apprenants.

Une première étape peut consister à faire découvrir le document en créant une activité interactive basée sur la recherche d'informations.

Dans un deuxième temps, on peut envisager un *brainstorming* lexical, sous forme d'arborescence, afin de faire émerger le lexique de base et la problématique propres aux biotechnologies.

doc. 3, 4 Ces textes permettent de se familiariser avec la notion de biotechnologie et ses éventuels débouchés. Leur exploitation a pour objectif l'acquisition d'un lexique spécifique ainsi que la réactivation d'outils linguistiques nécessaires à la réalisation de la tâche finale (comparatifs, superlatifs). Leur étude doit être précédée d'une phase d'anticipation qui peut consister à répondre à la question contenue dans le titre du document 3 et, éventuellement, à s'entraîner à poser de nouvelles questions sur le sujet.

doc. 5 Cet article, qui traite plus particulièrement de l'amélioration des plantes, compare la notion de culture sélective à celle de manipulation génétique. Cette comparaison peut être pour la classe l'occasion de recueillir les premiers arguments sur le thème à traiter et de s'entraîner à l'expression de la comparaison, de l'atténuation, du contraste et de l'opposition.

doc. 6 à 10 Cet ensemble de documents présente deux sortes d'arguments contraires liés aux OGM. Les documents 6 et 7 s'intéressent principalement aux aspects positifs des OGM tandis que les documents 8, 9 et 10 s'attachent à mettre en avant leurs aspects négatifs. Leur étude a pour principal but de relever, sous forme d'un tableau à deux entrées (*pros and cons*), les principaux arguments nécessaires à la mise en place du débat contradictoire prévu en tâche finale. Une étude par groupes avec restitution orale en classe entière peut être envisagée pour l'ensemble ou une partie des documents, exception faite du document 10 dont la complexité nécessite l'utilisation de la fiche d'aide à la compréhension disponible sur le site compagnon (doc. 10bis et doc. 10ter).

TÂCHE FINALE

Sur désignation de l'enseignant, les apprenants sont répartis dans les deux groupes suivants :
Those who are in favour of Genetically Modified Organisms (quatre à cinq apprenants).
Those who are against Genetically Modified Organisms (quatre à cinq apprenants).

Un temps de préparation suffisant doit être accordé à chaque groupe.
La durée de chaque débat n'excède pas quinze minutes.

Le débat est répété deux fois afin que tous les apprenants de la classe puissent y participer. L'enseignant veille à l'équilibre des groupes en fonction des savoir-faire et des savoir-être des apprenants. Les apprenants ayant acquis ou étant en passe d'acquérir le niveau B1 interagissent dans le premier débat. Ceux qui n'ont pas encore atteint ce niveau participent au deuxième débat dans lequel ils peuvent intervenir en imitant leurs camarades.

ÉTUDE D'UN PRODUIT

TÂCHE FINALE

À votre retour d'un stage dans une exploitation viticole aux États-Unis, vous êtes chargé(e) de présenter, en un court exposé de dix minutes, tout ce que vous avez appris sur la production de vin dans ce pays et sur le processus de fabrication du vin rouge.

ACTIVITÉ LANGAGIÈRE

Expression orale en continu

NIVEAU VISÉ

A2/B1

CAPACITÉS À METTRE EN ŒUVRE

⚙ Comprendre l'essentiel d'une information technique concernant un produit.

⚙ Trouver les informations pertinentes dans un document.

⚙ Présenter un lieu.

⚙ Décrire un produit.

⚙ Décrire une image, un tableau, un schéma.

It's all in the grape...

 BOÎTE À OUTILS

Quantifier	Adjectifs cardinaux	They produce 100,000 bottles of wine a year.
	Quantifieurs	Many different types of wine are produced in California.
		Very few winegrowers harvest by hand.
Comparer	Comparatifs et superlatifs	He produces less wine than his neighbour.
		The most prestigious Californian wine is called Opus One.
		This wine is lighter/stronger than the one we had before.
Situer dans le temps	Le prétérit	Jean-Louis Vignes planted the first European wine grapes in Los Angeles in 1833.
Rendre compte d'un processus de fabrication	Le passif	The grapes are harvested in September.
		The wine is transferred into oak barrels for maturation.
Expliquer/ illustrer	Outils de présentation et d'organisation du propos	To begin with, … Then, … Finally, …

1

Thomas Jefferson, father of Virginia Wine

While Thomas Jefferson is best known as the third President of the United States, Minister to France and Secretary of State, he was also the second Vice President, Virginia Governor, an inventor, wine connoisseur, gastronome, avid writer and vineyard operator. His role in promoting grape growing and wine in the United States is probably his least known accomplishment, but one of significance to US vineyards. Jefferson's views on wine are supported by many of his quotes such as this one: [...]

We could in the United States make as great a variety of wines as are made in Europe, not exactly the same kinds, but doubtless as good.

Origin: © Copyright M. Dillard, Wordscriber LLC

2

Welcome to Napa Valley

Origin: cc by R. Patel

3

American wine

American wine has been produced for over 300 years. Today, wine production is performed in all fifty states, with California leading the way in wine production followed by Washington State, Oregon and New York. The United States is the fourth largest wine producing country in the world after France, Italy, and Spain. The production in the U.S. State of California alone is more than double of the production of the entire country of Australia.

The North American continent is home to several native species of grape, including *Vitis labrusca, Vitis riparia, Vitis rotundifolia, Vitis vulpina,* and *Vitis amurensis,* but it was the introduction of the European *Vitis vinifera* by European settlers that led to the growth of the wine making industry. With more than 1,100,000 acres (4,500 km²) under vine, the United States is the fifth most planted country in the world after France, Italy, Spain and Turkey.

Origin: cc by-sa Wikipedia,
http://en.wikipedia.org/wiki/American_wine

4

Origins of California wine

The first grape vines were planted in California's soil in the late 1700's by Mexican missionaries. This first grape vine was an early Mexican variety that became known as the Mission grape. This was the most prominent grape variety in California until 1880.

[...]

Jean-Louis Vignes is credited with planting the first European wine grapes in Los Angeles in 1833. Originally from Bordeaux, France and trained in œnology in Paris, he established the first commercial winery in California and was also the first to export wine.

In the 1850's and 1860's, a bold and creative Hungarian soldier, merchant and political exile named Agoston Haraszthy [...] moved to California and began planting grape vines. He went on to collaborate with the American government and imported over 165 cuttings from some of the best European vineyards to California.

Haraszthy also dug caves for cellaring [...], promoted hillside planting, suggested the use of redwood for barrels when oak was not available and founded Buena Vista Winery in an area of Sonoma called Valley of the Moon.

Origin: © International restaurant consultant A. Allen,
www.aaronallen.com

It's all in the grape...

5

Winemaking during prohibition

During Prohibition, large numbers of people began making their own alcoholic beverages at home. To do so, they often used bricks of wine, sometimes called blocks of wine. To meet the booming demand for grape juice, California grape growers increased their area about 700 % in the first five years of prohibition. The juice was commonly sold as "bricks or blocks of Rhine Wine", "blocks of port", and so on along with a warning: "After dissolving the brick in a gallon of water, do not place the liquid in a jug away in the cupboard for twenty days, because then it would turn into wine".

Origin: cc by-sa Wikipedia
http://en.wikipedia.org/wiki/American_wine

6

The story of Robert Mondavi

7

U.S. may overtake Italy as World's biggest wine drinkers

Global wine consumption, on the rise in past years, is forecast to continue to grow in the coming ones, with the United States overtaking Italy as the world's biggest consumer by 2012, according to a new report [...] by the International Wine and Spirit Record.

[...] It predicted that the financial and economic crisis affecting many wine-consuming countries worldwide would only have "limited" consequences for the growth of the wine sector. [...]

Global production and consumption are both expected to rise, the report said, with production expected to grow by 3.83 per cent from 2008-2012 to slightly over 3 billion 2.4-gallon (9-liter) cases.

[...] In 2007, Italy overtook France, its wine-producing neighbor, to claim the title, buying 299 million cases, the report said. Based on past and current trends, it forecast that U.S. consumers would buy a total of 313 million cases in 2012.

Americans are already spending more on wine than any other nation. In 2007, the U.S. invested nearly $22 billion in wine purchases, the report by the London-based wine market research company said.

J. Barchfield, 01.13.09

Origin: © 2010 HuffingtonPost.com, Inc.

8

U.S. wine consuption and exports

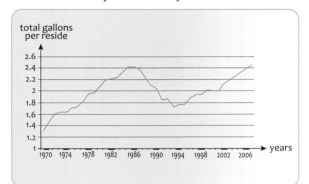

Wine consumption in the U.S.

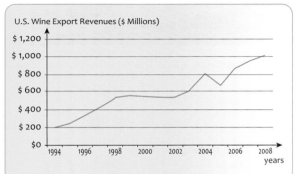

U.S. wine export revenues ($ Millions)

Adapted from: Exvere Inc. 2010

9

California winemakers "Going green" with sustainable vineyards

Wine grape farming and winemaking in California is a significant and growing part of that state's multi-billion dollar a year agricultural economy. And the vintners in northern California's Napa Valley have been among the first of the region's farmers to "go green" – leading the way in environmentally-sustainable grape growing and winemaking methods.

[...] Many traditional commercial farmers use toxic chemical pesticides to control the insects that feed on their crops. But Steve Honig of the Honig Vineyard and Winery tries to distract, rather than poison, the pests by planting thick hedgerows of tasty native plants just beyond the perimeter of his vineyard.

Like many sustainable vineyards, the Honigs also create habitats for insect-loving birds such as bluebirds. They also use bats and owls [...] to control the larger rodents that hide among the vines

The Honig Vineyard has invested heavily in solar technology. Solar panels convert sunlight into enough electricity to meet all the farm's electricity needs, from the wine cooling systems and air conditioners to the vineyard's lighting, irrigation pumps, and computer equipment. [...]

Along with sustainable energy, water conservation is an increasingly critical concern throughout the American West. Sustainable vineyards have now mostly replaced the flood irrigation systems of the past with drip irrigation methods, where tubes with small holes drip water directly onto the plant's roots in a controlled way, as needed. [...]

"When you can grow a good product using sustainability and it increases the quality of the product, that is a good showpiece for the rest of the world", he says.

Origin: © VOA Special English

10

Sustainable vineyard

Origin: cc by M. Smith

11

The wine making process

12

How is wine made?

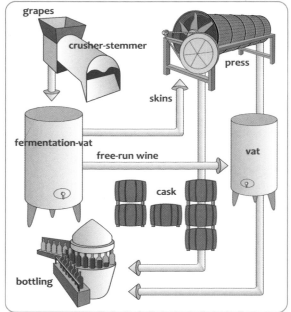

Adapted from: Napa Valley Vitners

PISTES PÉDAGOGIQUES

doc. 1, 2   Ce texte et cette photo ont pour fonction d'introduire la thématique de l'unité et de préparer à la lecture des documents suivants. À cette fin, il peut être intéressant d'amener les apprenants à formuler une série de questions sur la viticulture américaine, qui sont alors listées au tableau et trouvent leurs réponses au cours de l'étude des documents de cette unité. Ces questions peuvent également aider par la suite à la structuration de l'exposé prévu en tâche finale.

doc. 3   Ce bref historique de la viticulture aux États-Unis se prête à la manipulation d'adjectifs cardinaux, quantificateurs et comparatifs. L'occasion peut être saisie de comparer les données chiffrées à celles d'autres pays producteurs de vins, à l'aide, notamment, de recherches sur Internet.

doc. 4, 5, 6   L'objectif de ces trois documents est de permettre aux apprenants d'alimenter l'exposé final en relevant des informations supplémentaires sur l'histoire de la viticulture aux États-Unis et plus précisément sur son expansion en Californie. Ces informations peuvent être réorganisées chronologiquement sous forme d'une frise dont le commentaire oral conduit alors les apprenants à la manipulation du prétérit. Le document sonore doit être exploité à partir d'une fiche d'aide à la compréhension disponible sur le site compagnon (doc. 6bis et doc. 6ter).

doc. 7   Cet article, qui traite plus particulièrement de la consommation de vin aux États-Unis, permet la mise en place d'un lexique spécifique à réutiliser lors de l'exploitation des graphiques du document 8.

doc. 8   Ces deux graphiques peuvent servir de support à la première partie de l'exposé.

doc. 9, 10   Ce texte et cette photo abordent un aspect nouveau de la viticulture californienne. Il ne sont accessibles aux apprenants qu'après l'élucidation du lexique et la mise à disposition d'une fiche d'aide à la compréhension conçue par l'enseignant (en fonction du niveau de la classe).

doc. 11, 12   Ces deux documents présentent un aspect plus technique du thème étudié. Utilisés conjointement, ils doivent permettre de faire acquérir l'essentiel du lexique lié au processus de transformation du raisin en vin. Les outils langagiers nécessaires à la description de ce processus sont mis en œuvre à travers l'exploitation du document sonore (doc. 11).

TÂCHE FINALE

Les apprenants réalisent, en binômes, un exposé oral en anglais portant d'une part, sur la viticulture aux États-Unis et, d'autre part, sur le processus de fabrication du vin rouge.

La première partie de l'exposé doit être réalisée à partir d'un plan, accompagné éventuellement de mots-clés et de données chiffrées (l'utilisation de notes rédigées est à exclure). Le schéma du document 11 doit servir de support à l'élaboration de la deuxième partie de l'exposé.

Chaque partie de l'exposé n'excède pas cinq minutes.

Ce travail peut donner lieu à une évaluation.

Thème 4

PRODUCTIONS BIOLOGIQUES

TÂCHE FINALE

Vous êtes agriculteur(trice), engagé dans des pratiques respectueuses de l'environnement. En présentant votre travail, vous essayez de convaincre des touristes européens, de passage dans votre région, qu'ils doivent acheter vos produits issus de l'agriculture biologique ou durable.

ACTIVITÉ LANGAGIÈRE

Expression orale en continu et en interaction

NIVEAU VISÉ

B1+

CAPACITÉS À METTRE EN ŒUVRE

⚙ Décrire simplement.

⚙ Aborder et soutenir sans préparation une conversation.

⚙ Comparer et opposer des alternatives.

⚙ Exprimer et réagir à un point de vue.

Mother nature

  BOÎTE À OUTILS

Qualifier	Adjectifs épithète et attribut	The food smells good. He's got beautiful sheep.
	Adverbes	She really looks after her animals. He is always alone. We'll never be there on time.
	Mots composés	It's an eight-week chicken. Did you know it was pasture-raised? She's really good-looking.
Comparer	Le comparatif	Eat as much as you can. She is similar to a… The blue one's larger than the black. And now my farm is much more pleasant to work in.
	Le superlatif	Well, it was the worst meat I've ever eaten. Buying local would be the cheapest. That's the best news I've heard for a long time. Which is the most common practice? It's the least you can do.
Démontrer/ justifier/ persuader	Articulations du discours	Because / But / For / For that reason / So / So that / In order to / Therefore. The reason is… The thing is… The shop was closed for repairs.
	Relations logiques (cause, conséquence, but)	Thanks to / In order to / Due to / Because of / Since. Arrange things so that you finish tomorrow. Eat it quickly so it keeps its flavour.
	Énoncés complexes	That's what I said but my partner just wouldn't have it.

1

A sign on a farm

Origin: © 2007 by Joel Salatin & Polyface, Inc.

2

Polyface

Pastured broilers

We use 10 ft. X 12 ft. X 2 ft. high floorless, portable field shelters housing about 75 birds each to grow these 8-week meat birds. Moved daily to a fresh pasture paddock, these birds receive fresh air, exercise, sunshine, and all the genetically modified organism-free (GMO-Free) local grain they want. Integrating the cows to mow ahead of the shelters shortens the grass and encourages ingestion of tender, fresh sprouts. At Polyface, we want every animal to eat as much salad (green material) as its full genetic potential will allow.

Pastured eggs

An Eggmobile follows the cows in their rotation. The Eggmobile is a 12 ft. X 20 ft. portable henhouse and the laying hens free range from it, eating bugs and scratching through cattle droppings to sanitize the pasture just like birds in nature that always follow herbivores as biological cleansers.

Origin: © 2007 by Joel Salatin & Polyface, Inc.

3

Pasture-raised animals

Truly sustainable livestock farming requires the use of a pasture-based system. Pasture-raised animals roam freely in their natural environment where they're able to eat nutritious grasses and other plants that their bodies are adapted to digest. [...]

Animal health benefits

Animals raised on pasture enjoy a much higher quality of life than those confined within factory farms. [...] Pasture-raised animals also enjoy a diet free of the unnatural feed additives routinely administered on factory farms. [...] On pasture, animals get all the nutrients they need from grass and forage (other plants), and some animals, like chickens, get additional vitamins and protein from eating insects.

Human health benefits

[...] Research indicates that pasture-raised meat, eggs, and dairy products are better for consumers' health than conventionally-raised, grain-fed foods. In addition to being lower in calories and total fat, pasture-raised foods have higher levels of vitamins, and a healthier balance of omega 3 and omega 6 fats than conventional meat and dairy products.

Environmental benefits

Pasture-based systems can help the environment, especially through fertilizing the soil and by reducing the amount of grain produced as feed. [...]

Keeping small farmers in business

When you buy pastured meat, you're not only taking a step to safeguard your health, protect the environment, and improve animal wellbeing, you're also supporting sustainable farming and the farmers who choose to practice it. Small, local family farmers are invaluable members of the nation's rural communities and play a key role as stewards of the land. [...]

Did you know?

• Raising grain-fed cattle is extraordinarily resource-intensive; a cow must consume about 8 pounds of grain in order to yield one pound of meat.

• It is estimated that 12 to 32 % of all feedlot cattle develop liver abscesses as a result of the high-grain diet.[viii]

• If you, like the average American, eat 67 pounds of beef per year, then switching from conventional beef to pastured beef would reduce your yearly calorie intake by 16,642 calories![ix]

viii. Nagaraja T.G. and Chengappa M.M., *Liver Abscesses in Feedlot Cattle: A Review, Journal of Animal Science,* Vol 79, 1. p 287-298, 1998.

ix. Robinson Jo., *Why Grass-fed is Best: The Surprising Benefits of Grass-fed Meat, Eggs, and Dairy Products,* Vashion, WA: Vashion Island Press. 2000, p 12.

Origin: Used with permission of Sustainabletable.org ®, www.sustainabletable.org, © 2003-2010 GRACE

Mother nature

4

Aquaponics: the answer to sustainable farming

The practice of aquaponic farming is not a new technology, it dates back to the Aztecs, but recently it has been re-discovered. Aquaponic farming combines the techniques of aquaculture (fish farming) and hydroponics (plants grown in water) to create the most sustainable food production system on earth. The system works by using a type of fresh water fish (usually tilapia or trout) that multiply in a water tank, then plants are grown on the water's surface. The relationship works perfectly between the fish and the plants. The fish produce waste in the water, and through natural bacterial processes, fertilize the plants, which in turn clean the water for the fish. The process is completely organic and sustainable for both parties. And the best part is that this system can be used on a small scale in your backyard, or for commercial production on large farms.

Origin: © Justine, www.socialearth.org

5

Preservation of soil quality

Maintaining soil quality is a major issue in organic farming.

Studies have analysed the differences between conventional and sustainable agriculture.

The table below shows some major differences.

Study over 20 years	Increase with sustainable/ organic farming
Activity potentials of microorganisms	+ 70 %
Organic matter	+ 20 %
Microbial activity	+ 15 %
Soil carbon and nitrogen	+10 %

These figures show that sustainable/organic farming maintains and improves soil quality and microbial biomass activity: conventional farming does not.

Adapted from a scientific report

6

Giving grasslands a rest

7

The difference between organic and sustainable

To distinguish between organic and sustainable, here are some comparisons:

Certification

Organic farms must be independently certified every year and approved by the USDA, while farms using sustainable practices do not require any official certification.[...] The best way to be sure about the growing practices is to buy directly from a farmer – that way you can ask questions if you are uncertain about the sustainability of his or her practices.

Animal welfare

Organic farmers need to give animals "access" to outdoors, but they can actually confine animals and gain organic certification with as little as an open door leading to a cement patio. [...] A farmer using sustainable methods might keep his or her animals indoors in bad weather, but the animals are given ample space to move around naturally. [...]

Size of the farm

For organic farming, there is no limitation on how many acres can be used to grow crops. Sustainable farmers plant crops in relatively small, mixed plots as a form of pest control and to build soil fertility.

Food miles

Organic food can travel thousands of miles before reaching your dinner plate, and certification does not take into consideration the use of fossil fuels used to truck food. Sustainable food, however, is distributed and sold as close to the farm as possible.

Origin: Used with permission of Sustainabletable.org ®, www.sustainabletable.org, © 2003-2010 GRACE

8

Energy and food security

Modern agriculture depends heavily on the use of fossil fuels. Most tractors use gasoline or diesel fuel. Irrigation pumps use diesel fuel, natural gas, or coal-fired electricity. Fertilizer production is also energy-intensive – natural gas is used to synthesize the basic ammonia building block in nitrogen fertilizers, and the mining, manufacture, and international transport of phosphates and potash all depend on oil. [...]

Irrigation, another major energy claimant, is requiring more energy worldwide as water tables fall and water must be pumped from ever lower levels. In the United States, close to 19 % of farm energy use is for pumping water. In some states in India where water tables are falling, over half of all electricity is used to pump water from wells. [...]

Food miles – the distance that food travels from producer to consumer – have risen with cheap oil. At my local supermarket in downtown Washington, DC, the fresh grapes in winter typically come by plane from Chile, traveling almost 5,000 miles. One of the most routine long-distance movements of fresh produce is from California to the heavily populated US East Coast. Most of this produce moves by refrigerated trucks. In assessing the future of long-distance produce transport in the face of shrinking energy supplies, writer James Howard Kunstler observed that the days of the 3,000-miles Caesar salad may be numbered. [...]

The most energy-intensive segment of the food chain is the kitchen. Much more energy is used to refrigerate and prepare food in the home than is used to produce it in the first place. The big energy user in the food system is the kitchen refrigerator, not the farm tractor. While oil dominates the production end of the food system, electricity dominates the consumption end.

With higher energy prices, the modern food system that evolved when oil was cheap will not survive as it is now structured.

By L. R. Brown

Origin: © Earth Policy Institute

9

Away from tilling

11

Sustainable agriculture

10

A cartoon by Ron Morgan

Ron Morgan

Origin: © www.CartoonStock.com

Mother nature

PISTES PÉDAGOGIQUES

doc. 1, 2   Ces deux documents constituent une introduction au thème. À partir de la photo du panneau (doc.1), les apprenants sont conduits à formuler des hypothèses sur les différentes *faces* de *Polyface*. Le texte qui suit illustre une de ces *faces*.

doc. 3   Ce texte, assez dense, présente les avantages d'une agriculture durable. L'enseignant doit prendre en compte la richesse lexicale de ce document en apportant une aide adaptée aux apprenants et en consacrant un temps important à sa découverte. Son étude peut être répartie sur deux séances.

doc. 4   Au-delà de la référence historique, le texte illustre, de manière simple, le concept d'agriculture durable. Sa compréhension est facile : on peut, par exemple, demander aux apprenants de réaliser un schéma qui représente les interactions entre l'eau et les êtres vivants qui la peuplent : poissons, plantes, bactéries.

doc. 5   Ce document porte un regard scientifique sur l'exploitation des sols en agriculture biologique. Comme le contenu du tableau est explicite, on peut demander aux apprenants de travailler en binôme, l'un disposant de toutes les informations grâce au document complet, l'autre ayant à compléter le tableau en questionnant son partenaire. Une colonne aura, au préalable, été effacée (la colonne des chiffres, par exemple).

doc. 6   Cet enregistrement sonore présente un exemple d'utilisation des sols plus respectueuse de l'environnement. L'enseignant doit veiller à adapter la longueur du document étudié au niveau de la classe, sachant qu'une étude *in extenso* serait de nature à démotiver les apprenants. À partir d'un montage audio adapté, on peut envisager une étude sur deux séances, la première portant sur *what experts say*, la deuxième sur *what farmers can do*.

doc. 7, 8   Ces deux textes apportent des précisions sur les notions d'agriculture biologique et durable. La prise en compte du paramètre non négligeable qu'est l'énergie est amplement illustrée dans le document 8, dont l'étude nécessite une aide significative de la part de l'enseignant afin que les apprenants parviennent à une compréhension satisfaisante des différents enjeux présentés dans les deux documents.

doc. 9   Cet enregistrement sonore peut être étudié avant les documents 7 et 8 si l'enseignant souhaite aborder les notions d'agriculture biologique ou durable à partir d'une analyse comparée. Comme le document est très riche, une fiche d'aide à la compréhension (doc. 9bis et 9ter disponibles sur le site compagnon) peut guider les apprenants dans le repérage de l'information pertinente au regard du sujet abordé.
Avec des classes éprouvant des difficultés dans la compréhension de la langue parlée, il est opportun de ne pas étudier l'ensemble du document en une séance. Selon le cas, l'enseignant propose de ne travailler que la partie traitant de *Conservation tillage* (en gras dans le script disponible en ligne) ou, si l'approche comparée entre dans son projet didactique, il peut étudier les deux parties *Tilling* et *Conservation tillage* (en italiques) sur deux séances, consécutives ou non. L'enseignant peut également supprimer les passages qu'il n'a pas choisi d'étudier.

doc. 10   Ce *cartoon* offre la possibilité de produire en classe une synthèse de ce qui a été étudié plus haut, les élèves ayant pour tâche intermédiaire (seuls, en binôme ou de manière collective) de remplir les chaudrons avec les termes caractéristiques de chacun des deux types d'agriculture.

doc. 11   Il s'agit d'une vidéo dont l'utilisation reste facultative. Selon l'intérêt des apprenants, elle peut permettre de réactiver des outils linguistiques acquis précédemment.

TÂCHE FINALE

La tâche finale nécessite une longue préparation et la constitution de binômes ou de groupes. Certains apprenants jouent le rôle de l'agriculteur, d'autres celui de touristes très demandeurs de précisions. À tour de rôle, certains apprenants jouent, tandis que d'autres les observent avec une tâche d'évaluation à réaliser sur les prestations de leurs camarades à partir de grilles de co-évaluation. Des sites pédagogiques, sur Internet, proposent ce type de grilles.

AMÉNAGER L'ESPACE NATUREL

JARDINS, GESTION DE L'ESPACE RURAL...

AMÉNAGEMENT DE L'ESPACE

TÂCHE FINALE

Vous rédigez un tract, à l'intention des touristes visitant votre région, les invitant à se renseigner très précisément sur les randonnées pédestres ou la pratique du golf près de votre ferme, village ou bourgade.

ACTIVITÉ LANGAGIÈRE	NIVEAU VISÉ
Expression écrite	**A2**

CAPACITÉS À METTRE EN ŒUVRE

⚙ Écrire des phrases simples reliées par des connecteurs simples, dans un texte articulé.

⚙ Décrire simplement et brièvement des lieux.

⚙ Apporter de l'information simple mais précise sur un sujet concret.

"Nature, to be commanded, must be obeyed"

Francis Bacon

BOÎTE À OUTILS

Qualifier	Adjectifs épithètes et attributs	The view looks great. It's a nice walk.
	Adverbes	You'll really love the scenery. He is always open. You'll never get lost.
	Mots composés	It's a three-star hotel. Did you notice he was left-handed? She's really good-looking.
Situer dans l'espace	Compléments, prépositions et adverbes de lieu	On your right… / On your left… / Behind you… I saw him at the station. You'll find it at the end of the brochure. It's right next to/in front of the bridge. You'll find it in the forest under a big tree. Take it back to our office. It's two miles away, you can't possibly miss it.
Donner des indications	Adverbes et locutions de temps, de lieu, de durée, de manière	When you arrive, drop in for a visit. Once inside, take the lift to the first floor. Give me a call after you've arrived.

1

Footpath

Origin: © Barry Samuels

2

The West Country

The beautiful area of the West Country has so much to offer the independent walker with its contrasting scenery. Some of our walks encompass the city of Bath, which offers some of the finest architectural sights in Europe with the Roman Baths, Bath Abbey and the famous Georgian Royal Crescent. As you leave Bath via the Kennet and Avon canal and travel on into the Mendips you will be pleasantly surprised by the beautiful countryside of the area and the fascinating heritage. We have planned the walks so that you can discover the rolling hills of the Mendips with the tranquil and serene landscape and stone walled villages. Underground the Mendips are honeycombed with caverns carved out of the limestone by the erosive power of the water over millions of years. From the summits of these hills you are able to absorb the spectacular panoramic views towards Exmoor, the South Wales Coast and Salisbury Plain. Travelling onwards the tracks and footpaths will take you over the dramatic limestone cliffs to the coast at Weston-super-Mare, a traditional English seaside resort. Our walks give you the opportunity to discover the magnificent Wiltshire Downs and our English Heritage with the beauty and mystery of such unique places as Avebury together with the conservation village of Lacock and Stourhead, famous for the National Trust house and garden.

Origin: © Bath West Walks

3

Footpath features

Some of the many types of footpath features

A footpath sign

This footpath starts from the edge of a country lane and the wording is "Public Footpath". In this case you will need to know, by using a map, where the path actually goes. This post and sign is made from wood.

A "Kissing Gate"

Its purpose is to give easy passage to people but, at the same time, act as a barrier to animals. To pass through you step into the "V" shape on the right allowing you to move the gate to the other post and so walk out the other side. Why the name? Well the story is that a man out walking with his lady friend can pass through first and hold the gate shut – demanding a kiss before permitting his lady friend to pass through.

[...]

A bridge

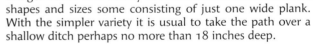

In this case the stream below is about 6-7 feet down so a substantial bridge is required. Bridges come in a variety of 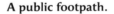 shapes and sizes some consisting of just one wide plank. With the simpler variety it is usual to take the path over a shallow ditch perhaps no more than 18 inches deep.

A public footpath.

Some are well used and, therefore, well worn as can be seen here. Others may be overgrown or less obvious and some, shall we say, can be a little more adventurous.

[...]

Believe it or not...

There is a public right of way across this field although it isn't obvious. If you look carefully you can see a track in the wheat, in the right half of the picture, where someone has crossed the field previously.

Origin: © Barry Samuels

4

Public rights of way

It is possible for landowners to allow access over their land without dedicating a right of way. These accesses are called permissive paths. To the user they are often indistinguishable from normal highways, but there are some important differences.

• A permissive path must have some sign or similar indication that it is not intended to be a right of way.

• The landowner can close off or divert the path if he wishes to do so, without any legal process being involved.

• The landowner can make restrictions which would not normally apply to highways, for example to allow horse riding but not cycling, or the other way around.

Permissive paths are commonly found on land owned by a body which allows public access, such as a local authority, a Railway Authority, or the National Trust.

Origin: © naturenet.net

5

Hedge planting – down on the farm

7

More trees on farms

6

Hedgerows

MARYLAND
DEPARTMENT OF
NATURAL RESOURCES

What are hedgerows?

Hedgerows are living fences of trees, shrubs, and other plants. A hedgerow can consist of a simple row of trees and shrubs or a pyramid of plant heights, from low grasses and flowers to tall trees.

Why are hedgerows important?

Hedgerows are tremendously beneficial to wildlife. In a hedgerow, songbirds, pheasants, quail, rabbits, and other wildlife can find food, shelter, and secluded passageways for travel from one area to another. With various levels of vegetation, from small flowering plants to shrubs to trees, an "edge" effect is created, providing habitat for more types of animals than one level of vegetation alone. Hedgerows can also serve as fences and they can establish contour guidelines for farming. Planting a hedgerow on the sides of your house that face the prevailing winds, can help you save energy. The same idea can be used to help save your fields from the wind erosion or heavy snow cover.

Origin: © 1995-2010 Maryland Department of Natural Ressources, www.dnr.maryland.gov

8

Golf course development

General

The last decade has seen 547 new golf courses opened in the UK, taking the total to 2,478, representing an increase in supply of more than 28 %. [...] There are 2.4 million golfers who on average fall in the 25-54 age bracket.

[...] Increased leisure time and activity holidays have led to a greater demand for golfing facilities. The type of facility required can vary from an 18-hole course, a 9-hole course, a par-three course, driving range, pitch and putt, or all of these combined in a full golf centre complete with club house and other leisure facilities. [...]

Market

Despite the large number of golfers, this venture should be looked into closely. The site must have good road access and be within easy reach of centers of population.

Physical requirements

[...] Site conditions: must be well-drained with natural contours and features, 10 % slopes are regarded as the maximum cross or uphill gradient on any length, but a flat site will not be favored either. The site should be sheltered and not exposed to snow or fog.

Origin: © SAC 2010, www.sac.ac.uk/diversification

9

Impact of golf courses

Advantages	Disadvantages
Employment and income benefits, both direct and indirect	Loss of biodiversity
Tax benefits to local, regional and national governments	Eutrophication or river or seawater through use of fertilisers
Attracts new firms to the region	Heavy user of water for irrigation
Health and social benefits. Careers can benefit through "networking"	Biocides use to maintain the greenness of the "greens", control insects, fungicides and weeds, contaminate both the air and water
Attracts the higher-spending social groups	Golf clubs often portray an elitist and exclusive lifestyle
Helps conserve valuable fragments of coastal habitat from encroaching urbanisation and agriculture	Leads to an increase in road traffic
Increases local property values	Raises property prices beyond the reach of local young people

Origin: With kind permission of Barcelona Field Studies Centre, http://geographyfieldwork.com

10

Golf course environmental impact

Message:

I live near a Golf Course and ever since it was built the health of a nearby creek has decreased dramatically. In the past it was full with fresh water that held fish, eels and turtles. There are now only puddles in which it would be impossible for an animal to live in. The Golf Course regularly pumps water from the creek and the creek beds are now covered in weeds, plant and trees because the lack of water has allowed the seeds to germinate and grow. Due to the lack of water less animals live in the area.

Golf Courses are generally considered "environmentally friendly" businesses but no one questions where the water comes from.

Submitted by Eva on 09.23.2009

Origin: With kind permission of Barcelona Field Studies Centre, http://geographyfieldwork.com

11

Countryside management – Plumpton

PISTES PÉDAGOGIQUES

doc. 1, 2 La photo, qui constitue le document 1, doit permettre à l'enseignant de présenter aux apprenants certaines facettes de l'aménagement. La richesse lexicale du document 2 doit faire l'objet d'un travail en profondeur et permettre l'acquisition du lexique de la géographie, de la campagne et de la nature.

doc. 3 Ces textes illustrés offrent la possibilité d'une comparaison avec ce que connaissent les apprenants, comparaison qui peut stimuler l'expression.

doc. 4 Ce texte permet, d'une part, de sensibiliser les apprenants aux différences de statut des chemins empruntés et, d'autre part, d'enrichir le champ lexical concerné par ce thème.

doc. 5 Cet enregistrement audio, au contenu historique et technique, ne doit pas poser de problème de compréhension majeur et permet de présenter un volet de l'aménagement : la plantation et la replantation de haies.

doc. 6 À partir de ce texte, l'occasion peut être saisie de faire réfléchir les apprenants sur le regard porté, depuis un demi-siècle, par le monde rural sur les haies et qui a conduit de l'arrachage à la replantation. Ce document fournit de nombreux outils lexicaux indispensables à la réalisation de la tâche finale.

doc. 7 L'exploitation de ce support audio doit être partielle, à cause de sa longueur. Elle peut s'articuler autour du rôle des arbres dans l'aménagement de l'espace. Une fiche d'aide à la compréhension peut être fournie par l'enseignant afin de guider les apprenants dans le repérage des informations essentielles.

doc. 8, 9, 10 L'étude de ces deux textes et du tableau permet d'acquérir les outils linguistiques nécessaires à l'évocation de l'existence d'un terrain de golf, outils à utiliser dans le cadre d'informations à communiquer à des touristes. La photo figurant dans le document 8 doit permettre à l'enseignant de faire s'exprimer les apprenants sur l'évolution de la pratique du golf.

doc. 11 Cette vidéo donne l'occasion de réactiver les outils linguistiques autour du thème de l'aménagement de l'espace. La bande son contient un message essentiellement publicitaire sur lequel l'enseignant peut attirer l'attention des apprenants, au regard de la tâche finale. La diversité des images peut permettre de stimuler la prise de parole, dans des tâches intermédiaires.

TÂCHE FINALE

Il s'agit d'attirer l'attention de touristes potentiels sur le cadre général des activités de loisir proposées et non de donner des renseignements précis sur telle ou telle activité. La production écrite nécessite sans doute une aide soutenue de l'enseignant, en particulier pour les aspects morphosyntaxiques. Pour stimuler la créativité de certains apprenants, la classe peut être encouragée à illustrer la production écrite ou le tract.

GESTION DE L'ESPACE RURAL, CYNÉGÉTIQUE

TÂCHE FINALE

La loi sur l'interdiction de la chasse à courre revenant dans l'actualité, vous avez été sollicité(e) pour organiser un débat dans votre commune afin de connaître l'opinion de vos concitoyens et de juger de la pertinence d'une campagne pour la modification de la loi.

ACTIVITÉ LANGAGIÈRE

Expression orale en continu et en interaction

NIVEAU VISÉ

B1

CAPACITÉS À METTRE EN ŒUVRE

⚙ Produire une courte synthèse orale.

⚙ Exprimer une opinion, des idées, des sentiments personnels.

⚙ Expliquer les avantages et inconvénients d'une solution.

⚙ Exprimer un accord, un désaccord.

⚙ Réagir à des objections.

Before shooting, one must aim

African proverb

 BOÎTE À OUTILS

Suggérer/ mettre en garde	L'expression de la suggestion :	
	– Modaux	You can't do that.
	– L'expression de la nécessité	We need to do it now.
	– La forme **V1 to V2**	She wants you to do it.
Rendre compte (de faits, d'événements, etc.)	Le prétérit	MPs voted against.
	Le **present perfect**	Fox hunting has always existed.
	Le discours indirect	Opponents say hunting is cruel.
	Le passif	The bill was passed.
Exposer/ illustrer/ donner des exemples	Outils de présentation et d'organisation du propos (introduction, exemple, énumération)	What I mean is… Well, to begin with, I'd like to explain what happened exactly.
Démontrer/ justifier/ persuader	Articulations du discours	The reason is…
	Relations logiques	Say it loud so that…

1

Going to the hunt

Origin: cc by-sa Sven Nissen

2

A typical fox hunt

The following is a generalised account of a pre-ban fox hunt.

Prior to a hunt the Master or huntsman would usually contact farmers and landowners in the area to agree where the hunt could go. The night before, or early on the day of the hunt, efforts were made to block up the entrances to fox earths, badger setts and places such as drains to prevent foxes going underground once the hunt has started. [...]

Usually, riders, hounds and followers met at about 11:00 am. The huntsman, hunt staff and hounds would go to the agreed starting point. The mounted field led by the Field Master, would follow at a distance. Followers would set off, in vehicles and on foot, to watch the hunt. [...]

The hounds would be encouraged to search for a fox in coverts, woods or rough ground. Once the hounds found a scent they would bark excitedly and follow the scent trail. Sometimes the hounds would catch a fox quickly and kill it before it could run. Other times, the hounds would pursue the fox. Often, the hounds would lose the scent so they might have to search in order to find it again. If the hounds were successful in their pursuit they would catch it, kill it and tear it apart. Some chases took just a couple of minutes whilst others could last half an hour or more. After a kill the huntsman or woman would call off the hounds, and then the tail of the fox, and sometimes its feet, would be removed and given to the followers.

Hunting with dogs has been outlawed in England and Wales since the introduction of the Hunting Act 2004.

Origin: © The International Fund for Animal Welfare (IFAW)

3

The Hunting Act

The Hunting Act 2004 is an Act of the Parliament of the United Kingdom. The effect of the Act is to outlaw hunting with dogs (particularly fox hunting, but also the hunting of deer, hares and mink and organised hare coursing) in England and Wales from 18 February 2005. The pursuit of foxes with hounds was banned in Scotland two years earlier under legislation of the devolved Scottish Parliament, while it remains legal in Northern Ireland.

Origin: cc by-sa Wikipedia, http://en.wikipedia.org/wiki/Hunting_Act_2004

4

Hunt the hunters

A rural lifestyle under attack

One of Tony Blair's less glorious achievements has been to provoke two protests of unprecedented proportions within one week of each other.
In 2002 there was first The Liberty and Livelihood March, organized by a group dedicated to preserving the rural way of life – The Countryside Alliance. With almost half a million people, it was the biggest demonstration in UK history until the Iraq war demonstrations surpassed it a week later.

Defending a way of life

By far the most prominent demonstrators marching for rural values were the ones dressed in red: the fox-hunters. When Labour came to power in 1997, it promised to outlaw fox-hunting. A profoundly urban political party, Labour has no idea how strong rural opposition to the ban would be. Although the British are a nation of animal lovers, in the countryside fox-hunting is not considered an example of cruelty to animals, it is a way of life.

Blair, like most British people, doesn't feel strongly about hunting, but the issue has shadowed his entire time as Prime Minister – parliament voted on it six times in the last seven years, with still no outcome decided.

Anti-hunt politicians recently forced a hunting ban into law by invoking an archaic parliamentary procedure that pro-hunt lawyers claim was illegal. Threatening civil disobedience that could affect the coming election, hunters have been able to delay implementation of the ban for two years.

Using terror to protect animals

Opposite the pro-hunters are the animal rights activists. Groups such as the Animal Liberation Front (ALF), the Hunt Retribution Squad and The Justice Department use extreme methods, including terrorism, to intimidate so-called animals exploiters, including butchers and laboratory researchers. By threatening the people who do medical research on animals, including their families and even the pubs were they drink, these groups make it impossible for labs to keep workers.
And their tactics work – the fur industry barely exists in Britain, several abattoirs have shut down, and medical labs are being forced to move abroad.

Oddly, while terrorism is being used successfully by activist groups, the government is using the threat of terrorism to attack civil liberties like never before.

R. Murdoch

Origin: © Bayard Presse/Today in English, April 2005

5

I'm sad that hunting with hounds will be banned

Grace has been going on hunts since she was very young and in her report she tells us why she thinks the hunting with hounds shouldn't be banned.

"I've been hunting for seven years – ever since I was three years old!
I really enjoy it. I get to see my friends, I'm out in the fresh air seeing beautiful countryside and it's good exercise.
I especially love galloping and jumping!
I normally go on a hunt every Saturday, it starts at 11.00 am and finishes around 4.30 pm. And we do it in all kinds of weather – it's a lot of fun when it's wet and muddy.

Don't understand

I'm very sad that hunting with hounds is now banned. It's something I enjoy and have been doing for so long.
I don't think that people against hunting understand what it's really all about.
It's about much more than killing a fox. It's very exciting to be riding with lots of other riders, it's a great atmosphere.

Old foxes

The foxes that do get killed are usually the very old ones, often with diseases. People also say that the foxes get ripped apart by the hounds and this is not true.
I believe that without hunting, farmers will be shooting foxes instead and this means that young ones will now also be killed.

Keep riding

I really hope that the ruling is overturned but I don't know if that will happen.
It's a shame that I won't be able to do something that I really enjoy. I think my pony will miss it too.
But I will still keep riding as I love going to pony club also."

Grace, 10, Herefordshire.

Origin: © from BBC News at bbc.co.uk/news

7

What is Britain without the hunt?

The English passion for horses [...] may be compared to the culturally entrenched American love of guns. Mirroring the conflicted British attitude to fox hunting, millions of Americans actually loathe firearms, and see them as an archaic vestige of a more primitive time. Yet the issue has been debated to a decision in Britain, while in America few politicians dare set foot in the quicksand of gun control. In the United States, a nation created through revolution, government encroachments on the right to bear arms is a dog that just won't hunt.

National Post, September 22, 2004.

Origin: © B. Kay

6

Arguments For Fox Hunting

"It's Traditional"

Fox hunting became popular in the 18th century. Before that, hunting hares, wild deer and wild boars were the main blood sports in Britain, but the extinction of the wild boars and the almost extinction of wild deer turned attention to foxes instead. [...]

"Hunting Gives Jobs"

According the League Against Cruel Sports (LACS), hunting provides jobs for around 750 people. [...]

"Meat Eaters Shouldn't Oppose Hunting"

Hunters claim that if you eat meat, you have no right to offer arguments against hunting. As far as they are concerned, meat eaters who oppose hunting are hypocritical. [...]

"The Animals don't Suffer"

[...]

"Foxes Terrorise the Countryside"

[...] foxes are a nuisance and run amok in rural areas, killing and maiming large numbers of chicken and lamb.

Origin: © RuralSports 2000-2011

8

Social life and class issues in the UK

Oscar Wilde, in his 1893 play *A Woman of No Importance*, once famously referred to "the English country gentleman galloping after a fox" as "the unspeakable in full pursuit of the uneatable". Even before the time of Wilde, much of the criticism of fox hunting has been couched in terms of social class. They argue that while more "working class" blood sports such as cock fighting and badger baiting were long ago outlawed, fox hunting persists, although this argument can be countered with the fact that hare coursing, a more "working class" sport was outlawed simultaneously to fox hunting with hounds in the UK. Philosopher Roger Scruton believes that the analogy with cock fighting and badger baiting is unfair because these sports were more cruel and did not involve any element of pest control.

Origin: cc by-sa Wikipedia, http://en.wikipedia.org/wiki/Fox_hunting#Social_life_and_class_issues_in_the_UK

No. VIII.
MR. BRIGGS HAS ANOTHER DAY WITH THE HOUNDS

9

Hunt saboteurs

"The disagreeable in full pursuit of the deplorable."

Origin: © www.CartoonStock.com

11

How many livelihoods at stake?

The kennels of the Cotswold Hunt provide jobs and accommodation for seven people.

If fox hunting is banned, say the Countryside Alliance, they and their families will not only lose a wage, but also their homes.

There are approximately 1,000 people in the UK who are directly employed and housed by hunting in this way.

And the Countryside Alliance says that a further 15,000 full-time job equivalents will be affected by a ban. Farriers, feed merchants, vets, clothing manufacturers, grooms and saddlers will be among those who will lose some work, if not their job outright, says the country sports lobby.

[...] But the figure is wildly inaccurate, according to animal rights groups and a rural economy expert. [...] The Countryside Alliance is saying that people will stop riding if they cannot ride with the hunt. "That's just nonsense – people will continue to ride, just not with the hunt. Therefore, all the saddlers and blacksmiths and riding attire manufacturers will not lose their jobs. This is just another example of the pro-hunt lobby clutching at straws".

Origin: © from BBC News at bbc.co.uk/news

10

Fox hunting, extract from a forum

Colin, I can understand you being very angry and fired up about this subject. We all know that this is more of a political subject that one based purely on facts. It is emotive on both sides, and country folk don't always do themselves many favors by constantly banging on about how the townies should stay out of the country, they don't know what life is really like here, etc. Fox hunting is a public relations nightmare for the countryside. A group of middle aged, overweight men riding horses howling with delight as a pack of dogs tears a fox to pieces is not the image we want to portray if we are seeking public support for our industries. Whether there is any truth in this image is not the point, it is just the way we are perceived. In my opinion, and I am sure you will disagree, the hunts should have acted sooner and placed some form of voluntary ban on killing with dogs in order to win public sympathy and safeguard the future of the hunts in some form. If they had acted as self-regulators then we could have avoided the humiliation of being told what to do by people who don't understand. [...] Whether you agree with it or not, fox hunting in this country is no longer seen as being acceptable by the vast majority of people. If you insist on hunting after a ban is imposed then you will only do more damage to the rest of us. We will then be seen as "fat gits from the country who are happy to take all our taxes for their bloody subsidies but who aren't prepared to obey the law, and enjoy killing innocent little animals!" Not my opinion by the way, but that will be the reaction.

Origin: © Mad Contractor, http://www.fwi.co.uk/

12

Hunting Poll

Do you think theses activities should be made legal again?

	Yes, should be made legal again (%)	No, should not be made legal again (%)	Don't Know (%)
Dog Fighting	2	97	1
Badger Baiting	2	96	2
Fox Hunting	21	75	4
Deer Hunting	12	84	3
Hare Hunting & Coursing	11	85	4

Origin: © Ipsos MORI, IFAW Hunting Poll, 09.15.09

PISTES PÉDAGOGIQUES

doc. 1 Cette photo permet d'introduire la thématique de la chasse et de faire un état des lieux des connaissances et points de vue des apprenants sur le sujet.

doc. 2 Ce texte décrit le déroulement d'une chasse à courre. Il permet d'étoffer le champ lexical de la chasse (lexique lié aux hommes et aux animaux). L'enseignant peut demander aux apprenants de retracer la chronologie des différentes étapes de la partie de chasse relatée dans l'article.

doc. 3 Ce document définit la loi de 2004 interdisant la chasse à courre. Outre un travail sur le champ lexical, il peut permettre de comparer la législation en matière de chasse au Royaume-Uni et en France.

doc. 4 Ce document sonore s'intéresse aux troubles suscités par la loi de 2004. Avant l'écoute du document, l'enseignant amène les apprenants à réfléchir sur les réactions des partisans et des opposants à la chasse suite au vote de la loi. Ce texte est l'occasion d'aborder l'aspect sociétal du problème (partis politiques au Royaume-Uni, système législatif) et de travailler le champ lexical du conflit. Il est, par exemple, possible de lister et comparer les termes associés aux défenseurs de la loi et ceux associés à ses opposants.

doc. 5 Dans ce document, une jeune fille parle de son goût pour la chasse. L'étude de ce texte offre la possibilité de réutiliser les outils linguistiques permettant l'expression des sentiments, ainsi que les temps, comme le *present perfect* ou le prétérit.

doc. 6 Ce texte propose une liste d'arguments en faveur de la chasse, qui servent à la réalisation de la tâche finale. Un *brainstorming* à l'oral peut permettre d'anticiper quelques arguments avant la lecture du texte.

doc. 7, 8 Ces articles montrent que la polémique sur la chasse à courre n'est pas récente et que, loin d'être un simple problème d'actualité, la chasse révèle de profonds clivages au sein de la société britannique. À l'aide de ces documents, les apprenants peuvent réfléchir sur la représentation des classes sociales, sur les clichés.

doc. 9 Ce document iconographique est une caricature sur la polémique provoquée par l'interdiction de la chasse, qui permet une réutilisation du lexique vu dans les documents précédents.

doc. 10 Ce texte est extrait d'un forum de discussions. Il se prête à un travail sur le lexique et sur le registre du texte qui contraste avec la passion que suscite généralement le sujet.
TÂCHE INTERMÉDIAIRE : imaginer le message préalablement écrit par Colin (message d'origine) auquel répond ce texte.

doc. 11 Ce texte s'intéresse à l'argument économique avancé par les opposants à la loi interdisant la chasse à courre. L'enseignant peut demander aux apprenants de réfléchir à son impact sur l'emploi et de compléter la liste des métiers qui touchent de près ou de loin la chasse à courre.

doc. 12 Ce sondage permet de conclure sur un état des lieux actuel de l'opinion des britanniques sur la loi de 2004. On peut, par exemple, demander aux apprenants de répondre, à leur tour, à la question *Do you think theses activities should be made legal again?*, et comparer leurs résultats avec ceux du tableau.

TÂCHE FINALE

La classe est divisée en trois groupes, formés par l'enseignant : les défenseurs de la chasse à courre, les opposants et les médiateurs.
Un temps de préparation de vingt minutes en groupe est prévu avant la prise de parole en continu. Chaque groupe dispose ensuite de cinq minutes pour exposer ses arguments, que les médiateurs ont pour rôle de synthétiser à la fin de chaque intervention. Le rôle des médiateurs est également de demander des éclaircissements, si nécessaire. Après l'exposé de chaque groupe, un débat permet aux apprenants de réagir aux arguments du groupe opposé.

JARDINS

TÂCHE FINALE

Employé(e) pour l'été dans une jardinerie, vous donnez des conseils à des clients étrangers sur l'aménagement et l'entretien de leur jardin.

ACTIVITÉ LANGAGIÈRE	NIVEAU VISÉ
Expression orale en interaction	**B1+**

CAPACITÉS À METTRE EN ŒUVRE

- ⚙ Accueillir la clientèle.

- ⚙ Se présenter.

- ⚙ Savoir demander un renseignement.

- ⚙ Répondre à des demandes de renseignement provenant de la clientèle.

- ⚙ Savoir décrire, demander ou donner des informations et des explications sur un lieu.

- ⚙ Expliquer des travaux à réaliser.

He who plants a garden plants happiness...

 BOÎTE À OUTILS

S'adresser à quelqu'un	Formules de politesse	Hello / Good morning / Good afternoon.
	Outils d'amorce du discours	Welcome / Pleased to meet you / Nice to see you...
Interroger	La syntaxe et l'intonation des énoncés interrogatifs	How can I help you? Will your flowers be in the sun or in the shade? Do you have a lot of perennials?
Donner son avis/ conseiller	L'expression de la subjectivité	To my mind / In my view / It seems to me that / What I think is / On the one hand I think... but on the other...
	La modalisation	I would recommend heat-resistant shrubs. I would advise you to take your time. It might be a good idea to plant perennials. If I were you, I'd buy an appartment!
Suggérer/ faire faire/ mettre en garde	L'expression de la suggestion	I would suggest that you wait until spring. Why don't you buy a lawn mower?
	Modaux	You must get rid of unwanted growth in the planting area. You could use a hoe.
	L'impératif et l'expression de l'obligation	Don't use chemicals. Kill weeds by cutting out their roots. Regularly water your plants.
	L'expression de la nécessité	You'll need a lot of tools.
Situer dans l'espace	Compléments, prépositions et adverbes de lieux.	At the back of the house, there is a small garden. There are all sorts of plants around the swimming pool. We'd like to plant roses along either side of the stone path. Some plants grow better when next to each other.

1 The joys of gardening

"Barney has a black thumb!"

Origin: © www.CartoonStock.com

2 Plant arrangement

HOW ARE YOU ARRANGING YOUR NEW PLANTS – BY COLOUR?

ALPHABETICAL ORDER

Origin: © Chris Madden

3 The Glory of the Garden

Our England is a garden, and such gardens are not made
By singing : –"Oh, how beautiful!" and sitting in the shade.

Origin: Rudyard Kipling, *The Glory of the Garden*

5 Nancy, an American gardener

4 British society is frightened of gardening

The television presenter and novelist Alan Titchmarsh said Britain has a stronger tradition of gardening than anywhere else in the world. But generations of sitting in offices rather than working on the land means that people have become frightened of battling the elements or waiting for something to grow. Children are so used to meals from packets they do not know where vegetables come from. [...]

The former Gardener's World presenter is fronting a new campaign with B&Q, a British retailer of DIY and home improvement tools and supplies, to try to encourage Britons to spend more time in their gardens. [...]

He said that the threat of climate change had added to people's fear of nature, when it should be encouraging them to take action by growing a garden: [...] "now we want to know the positive things we can do like planting things and improving the environment. People should return to eating fruit and vegetables in season. Children should also be taught how to grow fruit and vegetables in school". [...]

Mr Titchmarsh, who was once voted as the sexiest man on television after George Clooney, also insisted gardening skills can even make you sexy.

"People see gardening as sexy", he said. "I think it is because dexterity is required. When you watch Jamie Oliver prepare a dish in the kitchen or even Rolf Harris paint a picture it is impressive. People appreciate skill in sculpting, painting, gardening and cooking. It is not me, it is what you do".

By L. Gray

Origin: © Copyright of Telegraph Media Group Limited 2010

He who plants a garden plants happiness...

6

Our gardening business

8

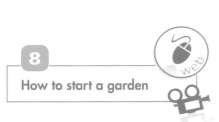

How to start a garden

7

Classifieds

Situation Vacant

Function: gardener
Hours: full time
Contract type: permanent
Location: Brighton
Ref: GJ1167

Skilled and passionate gardener wanted for a 25-acre park including lawns, beds, borders, rose garden, walled vegetable garden with large greenhouses and orchard. There is also a children's playground, a hedge maze and a lake.

Duties involve general maintenance including lawn mowing, weeding, hedge trimming, pruning, clearing leaves, turf cultivation, greenhouse care.

Candidate must have an NVQ3 in horticulture or equivalent qualification, a working knowledge of powered tools and previous experience in a similar role. Ability to work in a team is essential.

The hourly rate for this post is £10 to £12 depending on experience.

Apply online by sending CV and cover letter quoting reference GJ1167.

Adapted from a professional magazine

9

Before the buds break

Most gardeners know that the right time to start thinking about their spring gardens is as early as January or February.

Here is a list of things that need to be done before the planting rush:

– Buy seeds.

– Prepare your tools. Clean and sharpen blades (mower, pruners...).

– Clean your outdoor furniture.

– Prune all plants that require pruning (fruit trees, shrubs, woody plants).

– If any perennial has to be moved, this is the right time to do it.

– Get your plant supports and irrigation ready.

Adapted from a gardening magazine

10

Spring tasks

11

Gardener's forum

Hetty, Apprentice Gardener

Hi,

My family and I are just about to move into permanent accommodation for the very first time (yippeeee) and with it comes a garden.

At the front of the house there is a small strip underneath the window that we can plant [...], a very small lawn [...], and at the back a small garden with a shaded end over-looked by several trees.

There's not much opportunity to plant in the back garden [...] except for the fact that we have a charming stone path which I would ideally love to dig a channel along either side and plant up.

Problem is we are complete beginners! [...]

I would love to plant some pretty things in my small spaces, plants that look lovely, smell nice but don't need an awful lot of looking after and that will come up for more than one year.

I love things like lavender, rose, peonies, herbs, sweet peas, night scented stocks, etc. Nothing too formal. [...] We live up north [...] so it gets pretty rough here in the winter [...].

If anyone has any advice or thoughts, we would be very grateful for them, thank you!

Alice, Gardener

Hello Hetty and welcome to the forum.

I'm glad you've got your accommodation and a bit of a garden. You will be able to make it lovely. It's possible to do a lot with small spaces.

The year is quite far on now and what I would suggest to you is wait until you have moved in, take time to look at your space, see where the sun comes from and which areas are really shaded and windy. [...] Take time to think about it and come back here with questions. Come spring you'll be ready to make it just the way you want it. Good luck and enjoy.

Adapted from: Gardenerscorner.co.uk/forum

12

Friendly and courteous greetings

Customers are guests at your nursery and should be treated accordingly. The greeting [...] is perhaps the most important time you will spend with a customer. The confidence level you project is your first step for making a sale. [...] Make sure that your greeting begins and ends with a smile. Below are more introductory greetings:

"Good morning. How can I help you today?"

"Hello my name is _____. What can I help you find?"

[...]

After you greet your customer, ask [...] questions about the customer's needs or projects. Again, the questions should [...] require more than a "yes" or "no" response. Questions that find out who, what, where, when and why are the most effective. Consider the following example. A salesperson approaches a customer [...] looking rather confused:

Salesperson : "Hi. How can I help you today?"

Customer : "I'm looking for some flowers."

Salesperson : "I think we can help you with that. What area are you going to plant?"

Customer : "I'm planting a clay pot."

Salesperson : "Will it be in the sun or in the shade?"

Customer : "mainly in the sun [...]."

[...] The customer in the example above may need potting soil and fertilizer along with the plant for the clay pot. By asking the right question and recommending the right products, you will help customers complete their projects correctly [...] and enhance your credibility and the reputation of your nursery.

Origin: © 2008 Regents of the University of California. Used by permission.
Adapted from: *Retail Garden Center Manual* by D. R. Pittenger

13

Making the most of mulch

He who plants a garden plants happiness...

PISTES PÉDAGOGIQUES

doc. 1, 2, 3 Ces trois documents constituent une introduction au thème présenté. Ils offrent la possibilité à l'enseignant de faire l'inventaire du lexique dont les apprenants disposent sur le sujet.

doc. 4 Cet article dresse le constat du désintérêt grandissant des Britanniques pour ce qui, jusqu'alors, était considéré comme leur passe-temps favori. Son exploitation peut donner lieu à la réalisation d'un mini-sondage destiné à faire émerger les représentations que les apprenants ont du jardinage.

doc. 5, 6 Ces deux témoignages, sous forme de documents sonores, ont pour objet de familiariser les apprenants au métier de jardinier-paysagiste. Outre l'intérêt lexical qu'ils représentent, leur exploitation peut déboucher sur la réalisation d'une mini-tâche destinée à inciter les apprenants à se présenter et à évoquer brièvement leur environnement personnel, tout comme leur formation. Ces documents doivent être exploités à partir d'une fiche de compréhension, conçue par l'enseignant en fonction du niveau de la classe.

doc. 7, 8 L'exploitation de ces deux documents a pour objectif principal l'acquisition d'un lexique de base relatif au jardinage (tâches, outils). Le document vidéo permet, par ailleurs, d'entraîner les apprenants à comprendre une série d'instructions simples liées à une activité de jardinage et donne l'occasion de manipuler des expressions de la boîte à outils (suggérer et faire faire).

doc. 9, 10 Le texte et le document sonore visent à sensibiliser les apprenants aux travaux de jardinage à réaliser à l'arrivée du printemps. Ils permettent la réactivation d'un certain nombre de mots et de structures langagières étudiés précédemment, ainsi que l'exploration du champ lexical lié aux saisons.

doc. 11 Cet échange, extrait d'un forum dédié au jardinage, offre une nouvelle fois la possibilité d'observer et de manipuler les outils linguistiques nécessaires à la mise en œuvre de la tâche finale. C'est, pour les apprenants, l'occasion de s'entraîner à la pratique de la description d'un lieu spécifique tel qu'un jardin. Une des activités possibles est la réalisation d'un croquis du jardin décrit dans la première partie du document.

doc. 12 Ce texte, tiré d'un ouvrage professionnel à destination des futurs vendeurs en jardinerie ou en pépinière, sensibilise les apprenants à l'accueil de la clientèle. Son exploitation permet de réactiver les relations de civilité, ainsi que les énoncés interrogatifs.

doc. 13 L'utilisation de ce document est facultative. Son étude permet d'approfondir la connaissance technique et le vocabulaire des apprenants sur le sujet des jardins.

TÂCHE FINALE

Les apprenants travaillent par groupes de quatre : une équipe de deux vendeurs et un couple de clients débutant dans le domaine du jardinage.

À partir des structures, du lexique et des informations relevées lors de l'étude des documents composant cette unité, les apprenants doivent être en mesure de mener un échange portant sur l'aménagement et l'entretien d'un jardin.

Ce dialogue se compose d'un ensemble de questions posées par les clients et d'une série de conseils prodigués par l'équipe de vendeurs. Un croquis de jardin peut servir de support à l'activité. La durée de chaque conversation n'excède pas dix minutes.

PARCS NATIONAUX

TÂCHE FINALE

Employé(e) dans un parc naturel français, vous réalisez un panneau ou une affiche en anglais à l'adresse de randonneurs étrangers. Ce panneau présente des informations essentielles à leur sécurité, leur orientation, ou encore des notions de base sur la faune et la flore environnantes.

ACTIVITÉ LANGAGIÈRE	NIVEAU VISÉ
Expression écrite	**A2**

CAPACITÉS À METTRE EN ŒUVRE

⚙ Comprendre des consignes, des instructions.

⚙ Décrire un lieu.

⚙ Réaliser une affiche, un panneau.

⚙ Rédiger une série de consignes.

ᴨature lovers...

 BOÎTE À OUTILS

Suggérer/ faire faire/ mettre en garde	L'expression de la suggestion	Be careful.
		Please, stay where you are.
	Modaux	All refuse must be carried out.
	L'impératif et l'expression de l'obligation	Drink plenty of water.
		Don't let your children drink the river water!
		Never feed wildlife or bait animals for closer observation or photography.
	La forme **V1 to V2**	Black bears are fairly common in this region, so you have to be really careful on hikes.
Qualifier	Adjectifs épithètes et attributs	These animals are dangerous.
		The growing number of tourists poses a serious threat to the park's fragile ecosystem.
Donner des indications	Adverbes et locutions de temps, de lieu, de durée, de manière	When you arrive, drop in for a visit.
		Turn right once inside the park and follow the road to the end which will bring you to the parking lot.
Émettre des hypothèses	Propositions en **if**	If you see a bear, pick up your smallest child.

1

Attacked by a bear

Origin: © www.CartoonStock.com

2

National Parks

National Parks have been called "the best idea America ever had". The national park idea – the concept of large-scale natural preservation for public enjoyment — has been credited to the artist George Catlin, known for his paintings of American Indians in the early part of the 19th century. In 1832, while on a trip to the Dakota region, he was disturbed by the thought of the inevitable destructive effects of America's westward expansion on Indian civilization, wildlife, and wilderness. He thought they might be preserved by some great protecting policy of government, a nation's park, containing man and beast, in all the wildness and freshness of their nature's beauty!

During the 19th century, [...] men came West in order to trap, hunt, and otherwise exploit the land. Later, as wagon trains began to cross the continent in mass numbers, the fragile land was feeling the effects. As the wilderness receded and portions of prehistoric civilization were lost, some began to see the need to protect examples of the nation's heritage. [...] Spectacular natural areas in the American West were publicized, and the thought of preserving such places began to take effect.

One such spectacular natural area was Yosemite Valley. There, the "national park idea" came to partial fruition in 1864, when legislation was passed to transfer the federally owned valley, as well as the nearby Mariposa Big Tree Grove, to the state so they might "be used and preserved for the benefit of mankind". [...] It became a National Park on October 1, 1890.

By 1916 the Department of the Interior was responsible for 14 national parks and 21 national monuments but had no organization to manage them. To remedy this, President Woodrow Wilson approved legislation creating the National Park Service on August 25, 1916.

Origin: © 2001-2010 by Online Highways LLC. All rights reserved

3

Yosemite: one of the most famous parks in the US

4

Park ranger duties and responsabilities 1

Origin: cc by-sa L. Gohsep

Origin: cc by R. Scoble

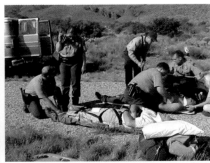

Origin: This material was provided courtesy of U.S. National Park Service. Additional information about U.S. national parks can be found at http://www.nps.gov

5

Park ranger duties and responsabilities 2

Origin: cc by OC Parks

Origin: This material was provided courtesy of U.S. National Park Service. Additional information about U.S. national parks can be found at http://www.nps.gov

6

Science careers: Park ranger

Nature of the work

Park rangers teach people to respect the delicate natural balance of our national and state parks and forests. [...] Rangers work throughout the country preserving the natural environment for future generations. They protect these areas by enforcing park rules and regulations, preventing forest fires, helping to maintain an ecological balance and seeing that visitors plan campsites wisely. Park rangers are skilled campers with a great deal of knowledge about botany and wildlife. Perhaps the greatest danger to our parks is the danger of overuse: rangers watch and regulate the number of visitors to parks. They also provide information regarding park use and points of interest, issue fire permits, and collect fees.

In addition to protecting natural resources, park rangers protect people. They may rescue a rock climber who has fallen or chase away a bear that is threatening campers. In addition, rangers act as educators by teaching campers how to use camping equipment, taking visitors on nature walks, setting up exhibits, and lecturing on historic topics. Park rangers also help to train new rangers.

Some rangers specialize in a certain type of patrol. There are backcountry rangers, who load up their mules with supplies and spend weeks at a time in isolated, undeveloped areas checking on hikers and watching for trails that need repairing. Snow rangers patrol their area on skis and are skilled in first aid, which includes applying splints to injured skiers. Some rangers make their rounds by boat or canoe [...].

Law enforcement is among the many duties of a park ranger. Some national park rangers carry guns. Park rangers sometimes recover stolen cars or quiet rowdy visitors. They are also in charge of investigating any suspected illegal activity committed in national parks.

Origin: © 2002-2010 Science Buddies. All Rights Reserved. http://www.sciencebuddies. org/science-fair-projects/science-engineering-careers/EnvSci_parkranger_c001.shtm

7

Hiker rescue

Animal attacks and mountain climbing accidents command the biggest headlines, but search-and-rescue teams are called out most often to help lost or injured hikers in America's National Parks. The National Park Service reports spending $3.5 million last year on 3,108 search-and-rescue operations – 1,264 of them to help hikers. [...]

One challenge for the National Parks: getting safety information to visitors to prevent emergencies. Some visitors come ill prepared, according to accident reports this summer. One elderly man who is legally blind and hikes alone has prompted search-and-rescue efforts in three National Parks. Last month in California's Lassen Volcanic National Park, he was lost overnight and, the next day, a search team found him with injuries he suffered when he left the trail and fell down steep slides. He also was dehydrated from packing just one bottle of water, records showed. [...]

While some people ignore warning signs, almost all visitors pay close attention if the warnings involve bears, said Laura Loomis of the National Parks Conservation Association. "People are very fearful of the bears, when in truth they are much more likely to get hurt from a fall or dehydration or drowning than they are by being attacked by a bear".

Origin: © G. & R. Mallery

8

Rules and regulation (Badlands National Park)

Your safety

– Summer is hot and dry. Carry and drink one gallon of water per person per day.
– [...] During lightning storms, avoid lone trees and high places. [...]
– Wear clothing and sunscreen to protect yourself from the sun. [...]
– Beware of the rattlesnakes that reside in the park. [...] Be careful where you place your hands and feet.
– [...] Watch for changing weather, and let someone know about your travel plans.

Protect your park

– Leave fossils, flowers, rocks, and animals where you find them. Collecting in the park is illegal. [...]
– Do not enter, alter or deface archeological sites. [...]
– All vehicles and bicycles must travel on designated roads. [...]
– Campfires are not allowed under any circumstances. [...]
– All refuse must be carried out.
– Hunting is strictly prohibited in Badlands National Park.
– Pets must be kept on a leash no longer than six feet at all times.

Origin: This material was provided courtesy of U.S. National Park Service. Additional information about U.S. national parks can be found at http://www.nps.gov

9

Safety considerations for parents

Big Bend is a wild and natural place with many opportunities to explore nature with your children. With a few simple precautions you and your family should have a wonderful time getting to know the park.

Have a first-aid kit handy

The Chihuahuan desert is full of plants that stab and stick; a fully equipped first-aid kit with tweezers can be very handy for extracting cactus spines from little bodies.

Drink plenty of water

In the dry environment of the desert, children's bodies use up water faster than adults. On any activity, pack along enough water for everyone. Soda pop is not a good alternative to water.

Don't feed the animals

It is a good idea to discuss with your children that the animals living in Big Bend are wild and can be unpredictable. Never allow your children to feed any animal. [...]

Mountain Lions

[...] While Mountain lions are rarely a threat to adults, young children who are unaccompanied by adults could be in danger.
[...] If you see a lion, pick up your smallest child. Keep all your children with you and stand as a group. DON'T RUN! Shout and wave your arms above your head. Mountain lion sightings are unusual and exciting, and most people see lions while travelling in their cars. [...]

The River

The Rio Grande is a surprisingly strong river [...]. Swimming is not recommended. Stay with your children as they explore the river shore, make them keep their shoes on, and don't let them drink the river water.

Origin: This material was provided courtesy of U.S. National Park Service. Additional information about U.S. national parks can be found at http://www.nps.gov

10

Wildlife viewing

Most visitors understand that feeding wildlife is against the law, but many people do not realize that disturbing park wildlife is also a violation of federal regulations and can result in fines and arrest. [...]

As a rule of thumb, if you approach an animal so closely that it changes its behavior, you have approached too closely. Instead use binoculars, spotting scopes and cameras with telephoto lenses to enjoy wildlife. Watch for any modification in an animal's behavior that indicates that you have approached too closely. Move away from the animal until you reach a distance at which the animal feels comfortable once again and resumes whatever activity it was engaged in before you approached.

Never feed wildlife or bait animals for closer observation or photography. Feeding park wildlife usually guarantees its demise.

Origin: This material was provided courtesy of U.S. National Park Service. Additional information about U.S. national parks can be found at http://www.nps.gov

11

Death in Yellowstone

∩ature lovers...

PISTES PÉDAGOGIQUES

doc. 1   Ce dessin humoristique permet d'introduire la thématique de l'unité. Son exploitation peut déboucher sur la réalisation d'un *brainstorming* lexical sur les parcs nationaux ainsi que sur les dangers que l'on peut y rencontrer.

doc. 2, 3   Cet ensemble composé d'un article et d'un document audio répond à un double objectif, qui est de véhiculer des références culturelles sur l'émergence du concept de «parc national» aux États-Unis et de se familiariser avec le lexique relevant des espaces naturels et de leur protection.
Le document 2, de par sa richesse lexicale nécessite un guidage important de la part de l'enseignant. Ce texte, ainsi que la deuxième partie du document 3, peuvent être utilisés conjointement pour dresser un historique des parcs nationaux à l'aide d'un tableau chronologique.

doc. 4, 5, 6   Cette série de photos et ce texte présentent les multiples facettes du métier de *Ranger* dans les parcs nationaux américains. Les documents visuels peuvent, selon le choix de l'enseignant, s'inscrire dans une activité de pré-lecture du document 6 ou, au contraire, conclure son exploitation par une activité de réutilisation et d'appropriation du lexique étudié précédemment.

doc. 7   Cet article, qui aborde les dangers susceptibles d'être rencontrés dans les parcs nationaux, se prête tout particulièrement à l'exploration du champ sémantique des accidents et de la sécurité dans les espaces naturels.

doc. 8, 9   Voici deux exemples de consignes de sécurité que l'on peut trouver dans les parcs nationaux. Ces deux documents permettent d'observer et de mettre en place les outils linguistiques indispensables à la réalisation de la tâche finale (impératif, expression de l'obligation et expression de la nécessité). Leur étude contribue également à l'enrichissement du lexique étudié grâce aux documents précédents.

doc. 10, 11   Ce texte et cette vidéo sont l'occasion de réactiver les outils linguistiques travaillés au travers des documents 8 et 9. À cet effet, il peut être demandé aux apprenants de reformuler les informations données sous forme d'une liste de consignes de sécurité.

TÂCHE FINALE

À partir de documents ou d'informations portant sur un parc national français, les apprenants réalisent une affiche ou un panneau à l'intention de randonneurs étrangers, dans lequel ils présentent brièvement le site et donnent des consignes sur la conduite à tenir dans ces espaces naturels protégés.
Les travaux doivent être effectués en groupes constitués de deux à quatre apprenants et sont affichés dans la classe une fois que leur réalisation est achevée. Ils peuvent donner lieu à une évaluation.

VOIR LES PRATIQUES ENVIRONNEMENT

BIODIVERSITÉ

TÂCHE FINALE

Vous appartenez à une association qui milite pour la sauvegarde de la biodiversité et, à l'occasion d'un événement mondial tel que la Journée internationale de la biodiversité, vous rédigez un message électronique invitant vos contacts à se mobiliser pour sauver une espèce en danger.

ACTIVITÉ LANGAGIÈRE

Expression écrite

NIVEAU VISÉ

A2

CAPACITÉS À METTRE EN ŒUVRE

⚙ Écrire un message électronique.

⚙ Décrire, en termes simples, un animal ou une plante.

⚙ Rédiger une série de consignes.

Variety is the spice of life

 BOÎTE À OUTILS

Qualifier	Adjectifs épithètes et attributs	The male is about 3 inches tall. They feed on insects and small invertebrates.
	Adverbes	Toads typically live 2 or 3 years.
	Mots composés	The black-footed ferret is threatened with extinction.
Rendre compte (de faits, d'événements)	Le prétérit	A disease ruined the crop for several years.
	Le **present perfect**	Scientists have identified about 1.75 million species.
	Le discours indirect	Experts say the world depends on only four crops.
	Le passif	Crops are pollinated by insects.
Démontrer/ justifier/ persuader	Articulations du discours	For that reason, we must limit the use of pesticides. The reason is…
	Relations logiques (cause, conséquence, but)	Pass this on to your email friends so that they get involved.
S'exclamer	Adverbes, expressions et énoncés exclamatifs	Act now! Get involved! Have a look at our website!

1

Noah's arch

"Hang on, hang on, what did I just say?"

Origin: © www.CartoonStock.com

2

Biodiversity is life

You are biodiversity. Most of the oxygen you breathe comes from plankton in the oceans of the world and lush forests around the globe. Your diet depends almost entirely on the plants and animals around us, from the grasses that give us rice and wheat, to the fish and meat from both wild and farmed landscapes. Your body contains up to 100 trillion cells and is connected with everything around you and the wider world in a wonderfully complex and timeless system. You share your atoms with every being and object in the natural world, you are both ancient and inconceivably young.

Origin: © UK National Commission for UNESCO

4

International Year of Biodiversity

3

E.U. campaign for biodiversity

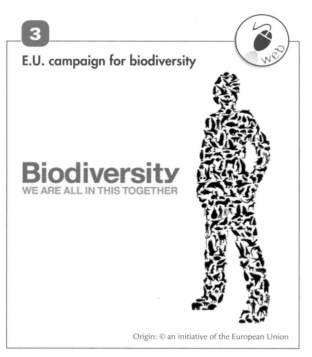

Origin: © an initiative of the European Union

5

Poster

Origin: © Biodiversity Month Project & Green Team Advertising,
photo © by S. Middleton and D. Liittschwager

6

Biodiversity and agriculture

Humans are directly dependent upon a variety of plants and animals that provide our supply of food. Furthermore, the production of these foodstuffs involves a variety of ecological processes and the activities of many different living organisms. Without biodiversity, none of our food could be produced. Here are a few essential agricultural processes made possible by Earth's biodiversity:

Pest Control

Natural predators such as wasps and birds help reduce populations of pests that destroy plants on farms.

Pollination

Many of the world's staple crops are pollinated by insects, birds, bats and other animals.

Productive Soil

A variety of living organisms take part in the decomposition processes that create soils and make nutrients available for plants to use.

Resistance to Disease and Pests

Genetic diversity helps to provide resistance to disease and pests – mass production of a single crop variety makes it easier for a disease or pest to wipe out the entire crop.

Unfortunately, industrial agriculture has caused a dramatic reduction of genetic diversity within the animal and plant species typically used for food. About 7,000 different species of plants have been raised as food crops in the history of human agriculture. Yet in part because of modern tendencies towards mass production, only fifteen plant and eight animal species are now relied upon for about 90 % of all human food[iii]. As a result of this homogenization of the food industry, thousands of noncommercial animal breeds and crop varieties have disappeared, along with the valuable genetic diversity they possessed. [...]

According to the Food and Agriculture Organization of the United Nations, since 1900, approximately 75 % of the world's genetic diversity of agricultural crops has been eliminated[xiii].

Origin: Used with permission of Sustainabletable.org ®, www.sustainabletable.org, © 2003-2010 GRACE

iii United Nations Convention on Biological Diversity, *Agricultural Biodiversity: Introduction*, 2005 (accessed October 12, 2006).
xiii Food and Agriculture Organization of the United Nations, *Special: Biodiversity for Food and Agriculture: Farm Animal Genetic Resources*, FAO, February 1998.

7

Agriculture report – importance of biodiversity

The idea of biodiversity recognizes that natural systems are complex and depend on one another.

In agriculture, depending on only a few crops can be dangerous. One example is the Great Potato Famine in the eighteen forties. Ireland depended on potatoes as a food resource. But a disease ruined the crop for several years. More than one million people died from hunger.

Yet experts say the world depends on only four crops to provide half its food energy from plants. These are wheat, maize, rice and potato.

The experts say it is important to support a large number of different food crops and farm animals that can survive different conditions. Such diversity helps to reduce the risk from losing one main crop.

Farmers also have a responsibility to protect wild species. The Food and Agriculture Organization says more than forty percent of all land is used

2010 International Year of Biodiversity

for agriculture. Farm fields are an important place for wild animals to live and reproduce.

Also, farmers must consider the effects that agriculture has on the environment. Farm pollution or poor agricultural methods can harm wetlands, rivers and other environments needed to support life.

The World Bank says invasive species are a severe threat to biodiversity. Plants and animals often spread without natural controls when they enter areas they are not native to. They can destroy crops, native species and property. Invasive species cost the world economy thousands of millions of dollars each year.

G. Outen

Origin: © VOA Special English

8

Species Extinction Rates

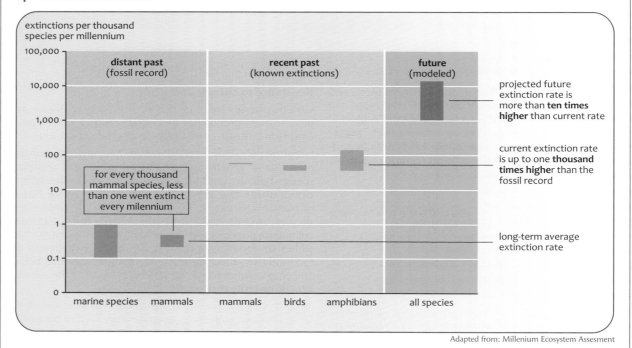

extinctions per thousand
species per millennium

distant past
(fossil record)

recent past
(known extinctions)

future
(modeled)

projected future
extinction rate is
more than **ten times
higher** than current rate

current extinction rate
is up to one **thousand
times highe**r than the
fossil record

for every thousand
mammal species, less
than one went extinct
every milennium

long-term average
extinction rate

marine species   mammals   mammals   birds   amphibians   all species

Adapted from: Millenium Ecosystem Assesment

9

The benefits
of biodiversity

10

The Eden project

11

Boy inspires planting of one million trees

At the age of nine, Felix Finkbeiner hatched the idea to plant one million trees in Germany. He did a presentation in his school about the idea and people listened. He was inspired by the example of Wangari Maathai, a Kenyan environmentalist who has helped organize the planting of 30 million trees. Felix wanted to plant one million trees in every country he could. Three years later, Germany has an additional one million trees, and Felix's organization called *Plant for the Planet* is doing work in 70 countries.

He made a great insight recently about climate change and the inability of bureaucracies to accomplish things in practical terms with swiftness. "We children feel really cheated because such a lot was done for Copenhagen and at the end, what was really achieved there?", Felix said.

The media picked up his story fairly early on, and the exposure has helped with donations. Also, his family has a strong environmental perspective. His father also started a conservation group, though not at such a young age. Today Felix is often invited to speak at conferences around the world. He keeps up with schoolwork but sometimes is away from home for weeks.

Plant for the Planet actually has a target goal of planting 212,000,000 trees. So far they have planted just over a million, and there are about 1.4 million pledged for planting. A humorous but pointed awareness campaign of theirs is called *Stop Talking and Start Planting*. Professional photographers donated their time and photos for the campaign.

Origin: © Care2, originally published at www.care2.com/greenliving

PISTES PÉDAGOGIQUES

doc. 1   Ce document iconographique introduit la thématique de la biodiversité et de la préservation des espèces.

doc. 2, 3   Ce texte et ce logo de la campagne de protection de la biodiversité menée par l'Union européenne définissent la biodiversité en montrant les interactions entre les organismes vivants. Ces deux documents peuvent être étudiés consécutivement, le texte apportant un lexique que le document iconographique permet de fixer.

doc. 4   Ce document audio aborde le sujet des dangers qui menacent la biodiversité. Il permet de construire un champ lexical spécifique au problème soulevé et de l'étayer grâce à des éléments factuels. Les apprenants peuvent construire une carte heuristique établissant les interactions entre les différents exemples cités dans le document. La vidéo complète de ce document est disponible sur le site compagnon.

doc. 5   Ce document iconographique est l'affiche d'une campagne pour la sauvegarde de la biodiversité menée par l'université du Colorado en 2002. Il peut être l'occasion de travailler la méthodologie de l'analyse d'un document iconographique et permet de réutiliser le lexique étudié dans les documents précédents.
TÂCHE INTERMÉDIAIRE POSSIBLE : les apprenants créent une affiche contenant un slogan mettant en évidence l'importance d'une espèce en voie de disparition.

doc. 6, 7   Ces deux textes, qui se complètent, soulignent l'importance des interactions entre la biodiversité et l'agriculture. Les apprenants peuvent construire une carte heuristique établissant ces liens de dépendance. Le document 6 permet en outre de revoir l'emploi du *present perfect*.

doc. 8   Ce tableau présente le rythme d'extinction des espèces et permet aux apprenants d'être sensibilisés à la menace qui pèse sur certaines espèces. Il complète l'étude des documents 6 et 7.

doc. 9   Ce document audio est la suite du document 4. Ce passage s'intéresse aux avantages que nous tirons de la biodiversité. On peut demander aux apprenants de lister les différents secteurs d'activité mentionnés dans le document et d'y apporter des exemples. La vidéo complète de ce document est disponible sur le site compagnon.

doc. 10, 11   Ce document sonore et ce texte sont deux exemples de mise en œuvre de projets visant à sauvegarder la biodiversité. Le document 10 étant relativement dense, il est souhaitable d'accompagner l'écoute d'une fiche d'aide à la compréhension.

TÂCHE FINALE

Les apprenants rédigent un courrier électronique qui doit contenir les informations suivantes :
– des formules de civilité et de politesse adaptées ;
– une présentation d'une espèce en voie de disparition ;
– une invitation à se mobiliser ;
– une pièce jointe ou un renvoi à un site Internet.

Thème 10

L'EAU

TÂCHE FINALE

Dans le cadre de la Journée de l'eau, vous réalisez une enquête sur la consommation quotidienne en eau de vos camarades et faites un compte-rendu oral devant la classe, en proposant des pistes pour faire des économies.

ACTIVITÉ LANGAGIÈRE

Expression écrite et orale en continu

NIVEAU VISÉ

A2+

CAPACITÉS À METTRE EN ŒUVRE

⚙ Produire un compte-rendu écrit.

⚙ Produire une courte synthèse orale.

⚙ Exposer des solutions et suggérer ou proposer des modifications.

⚙ Donner des informations sur des personnes, des actes.

Dirty water cannot be washed

 BOÎTE À OUTILS

Rendre compte (de faits, d'événements…)	Le prétérit	I realised that many people…
	Le discours indirect	Some people said they were not concerned.
Exposer/ Illustrer/ Donner des exemples	Outils de présentation et d'organisation du propos (introduction, exemple, énumération…)	This is a situation we can not ignore.
		To begin with, I'd like to explain the situation.
Donner son avis/ conseiller	L'expression de la subjectivité	I think it's OK.
	La modalisation	I don't like the idea of giving up.
		(I think) we should be more careful.
Démontrer/ Justifier/ Persuader	L'articulation du discours	The reason is…
	Relations logiques (cause, conséquence, but)	The thing is…
		In order to reduce our consumption…
Émettre des hypothèses/ Nuancer son propos	Expressions de l'atténuation	Opinion is divided but…
	Le conditionnel	This difficulty mustn't be overlooked, but…
	La valeur des modaux et la modalisation	We shouldn't…
	L'expression du futur	If we don't change our habit, we'll face severe problems.

1

World Water Forum in Mexico

Origin: © 2006 Frederick Deligne, Nice-Matin, France, and PoliticalCartoons.com

2

Areas of physical and economic water scarcity

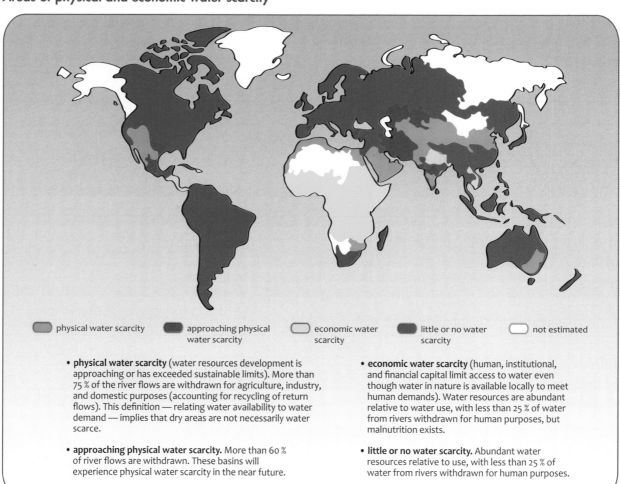

physical water scarcity   approaching physical water scarcity   economic water scarcity   little or no water scarcity   not estimated

- **physical water scarcity** (water resources development is approaching or has exceeded sustainable limits). More than 75 % of the river flows are withdrawn for agriculture, industry, and domestic purposes (accounting for recycling of return flows). This definition — relating water availability to water demand — implies that dry areas are not necessarily water scarce.

- **approaching physical water scarcity.** More than 60 % of river flows are withdrawn. These basins will experience physical water scarcity in the near future.

- **economic water scarcity** (human, institutional, and financial capital limit access to water even though water in nature is available locally to meet human demands). Water resources are abundant relative to water use, with less than 25 % of water from rivers withdrawn for human purposes, but malnutrition exists.

- **little or no water scarcity.** Abundant water resources relative to use, with less than 25 % of water from rivers withdrawn for human purposes.

Adapted from: © FAO, 2010 and Comprehensive Assessment of Water Management in Agriculture, 2007

3

Troubled Waters

A schoolgirl in rural Ethiopia. A city-dweller in Bolivia. A farmer in Sri Lanka. A factory worker in Romania. Different lifestyles, different cultures, one challenge: making sure they have adequate supplies of clean, safe freshwater to improve their lives. Whether they are struggling to grow food in a drought-stricken area or living downstream from a melting glacier, their communities are dealing with tough questions about how to maintain a precious and finite natural resource. Global water use is increasing at more than twice the rate of population growth and more people than ever are learning first-hand about coping with water scarcity.

Origin: © FAO, 2010

4

Global inequities in water use

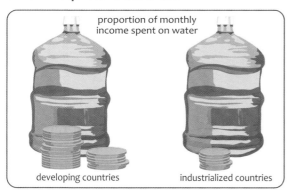

proportion of monthly income spent on water

developing countries   industrialized countries

In Africa, household water use averages 47 litres per person. In Asia, the average is 95 litres. In the United Kingdom the average is 334 litres per person per day and in the United States the average is 578 litres per person per day.
UNFPA (2002), water: a critical resource.

Origin: © FAO, 2010

7

Water, people and the future

5

Water quality: healthy people, healthy ecosystems

Water is the basis of life on earth. The quality of life directly depends on water quality. Good water quality sustains healthy ecosystems and hence leads to improved human well-being. However, poor water quality affects the environment and human well-being. For example waterborne diseases cause the death of more than 1.5 million children each year.

The quality of water resources is increasingly threatened by pollution. Human activity over the past 50 years is responsible for unprecedented pollution of water resources in history. It is estimated that over 2.5 billion people globally live without adequate sanitation.

Every day, 2 million tons of sewage and other effluents drain into the world's waters. The problem is worse in developing countries where over 90 % of raw sewage and 70 % of untreated industrial wastes are dumped into surface waters.

Origin: © FAO, 2010

6

Water for food

The ability to produce food is essential to reducing poverty and encouraging social and economic development. But increased agricultural production has come at a steep price.

Amount of water (litres) required to produce

1 kilo of grain-fed beef
15,000

1 kilo of wheat
1,500

Daily drinking requirements
2 - 5

While rainfed agriculture accounts for 80 % of the total cropland and irrigated agriculture accounts for 20 %, it is this latter that contributes to 40 % of the total food production. Still, irrigation has strained groundwater and surface water supplies, weakened the quality and resistance of the soil with salt deposits and water logging, and reduced naturally-occurring plant and animal species. The agriculture sector must take the lead in meeting a challenge that no one can afford to ignore – finding ways to do more with less water and reducing potential damage to the environment.

Origin and adapted from: © FAO, 2010

8

No access

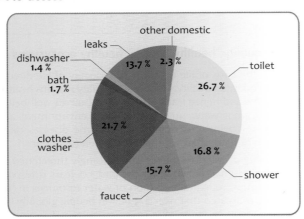

Typical Household Water Use

other domestic **2.3** %
leaks **13.7** %
dishwasher **1.4** %
bath **1.7** %
toilet **26.7** %
clothes washer **21.7** %
faucet **15.7** %
shower **16.8** %

In an industrialized city with plenty of water, flushing the toilet in an average household can send up to 50 litres of water down the drain every day. Yet more than one in six people worldwide – 1.1 billion – don't have access to 20-50 litres of safe freshwater daily, the minimum range suggested by the UN to ensure each person's basic needs for drinking, cooking and cleaning. Two people in five lack proper sanitation facilities, and every day, 3800 children die from diseases associated with a lack of safe drinking water and proper sanitation.

Access to clean water and adequate sanitation are part of the gulf that separates people who live healthy, productive lives from those who are unable to grow enough food to eat, earn enough income, resist life-threatening diseases and send their children to school. But the haves and the have-nots are all part of the same global fabric. The consequences of large-scale international problems like war and the spread of HIV/AIDS can be worsened by poor access to water and sanitation.

Origin and adapted from: © FAO, 2010

9

Going private: a recipe for success

California may be dry but Californians use more water than any other US state. Yet through government help, only a fraction of the costs of building dams, pumps and pipelines to supply water are passed on to water users in California.

Cheap water encourages people to waste it or pollute it. For example, land can become waterlogged as farmers over-water their crops. To avoid a crisis in the future, water must be privately owned and traded so that people pay the real price of water.

Already, new ways of owning and pricing water are being tested in California. In some areas, "water banks" act as trading houses where water can be bought and sold by private owners. The water bank changes the price of water according to demand and the amount of water available. Water prices can go up if people demand more water, and studies show that Californians will save water if prices are higher. After all, most people are not going to turn off the tap until they feel the pinch in their wallets.

Origin: © SOS Villages d'Enfants

10

Waste and restriction of water

Origin: © Copyright 2008 Arcadio Esquivel, La Prensa, Panama, and PoliticalCartoons.com

11

Water me worry? (cartoon)

12

Water worries

13

What do you do to save water?

Dirty water cannot be washed

PISTES PÉDAGOGIQUES

doc. 1   Ce dessin a pour but de contextualiser une vaste thématique, celle de l'eau, abordée dans un premier temps sous l'angle des disparités et des contrastes entre pays industrialisés et pays émergents.

doc. 2   Cette carte offre un aperçu du problème de l'accès à l'eau dans le monde. Outre la description du document, les apprenants émettent des hypothèses sur les causes de la disparité entre les pays industrialisés et les pays émergents.

doc. 3   Ce texte illustre le document précédent à l'aide de différents exemples.

doc. 4   Ce dessin et le texte qui l'accompagne soulignent les inégalités face à l'accès à l'eau (utilisation et coût). Les apprenants établissent des comparaisons, en prenant appui sur une carte heuristique élaborée à partir de leurs hypothèses, sur les raisons de ces inégalités.

doc. 5   Ce texte aborde le problème de la qualité de l'eau et de son impact sur la survie de l'écosystème. Les apprenants élaborent un tableau à double entrée permettant de séparer les bénéfices de l'accès à l'eau courante et les risques liés à une mauvaise qualité ou un manque d'eau. C'est l'occasion de réutiliser les outils linguistiques permettant d'exprimer les causes et les conséquences.

doc. 6   Ce document rappelle que l'eau n'est pas qu'une simple boisson, mais qu'elle est la base de toute une chaîne alimentaire, cruciale pour l'agriculture. Il permet de réfléchir sur les possibles conséquences du manque d'eau dans un avenir proche en utilisant des outils linguistiques tels que le futur, les propositions en *if*, le conditionnel…
TÂCHE INTERMÉDIAIRE SUGGÉRÉE : sélectionner une production agricole locale et lister les étapes où, dans la chaîne de production, l'eau est utilisée.

doc. 7   Ce document audio illustre la relation de dépendance qui existe entre l'eau et l'agriculture. Il pose le problème de la baisse des ressources en eau (eau de surface et nappes phréatiques) dans certains états américains et présente diverses solutions mises en œuvre pour pallier ces baisses. Le lexique et les informations contenus dans ce document aident à la réalisation de la tâche finale.

doc. 8, 9, 10, 11   Ces documents de natures variées offrent une vision critique de l'attitude des consommateurs dans les pays industrialisés, vision qui contraste avec le point de vue adopté dans les documents 4 et 5. Ils peuvent être l'occasion de travailler l'expression de la modalité.

doc. 12, 13   Ces textes comportent deux courts témoignages de jeunes adolescents sur la question de l'eau. Ils préparent à l'écoute des documents sonores les accompagnant. L'un se focalise sur les problèmes de sécheresse et d'inondation, l'autre traite des différents moyens existant pour économiser l'eau. Ils recentrent le débat sur le vécu des apprenants.

TÂCHE FINALE

En classe, les apprenants élaborent ensemble une fiche proposant différentes utilisations possibles de l'eau au cours d'une journée.
En binôme, ils réalisent ensuite leur sondage et rédigent un compte-rendu écrit contenant un diagramme synthétisant les réponses sous forme de pourcentages, expliqué par un court texte contenant des suggestions pour réduire la consommation en eau.
Ils présentent enfin ce compte-rendu à l'oral au reste de la classe sous la forme d'un exposé de cinq minutes.

Thème 11

ÉNERGIES RENOUVELABLES

TÂCHE FINALE

Dans le cadre de la semaine du développement durable, vous participez au concours de la meilleure innovation sur le thème des énergies renouvelables. Le but est de détourner un objet du quotidien et d'en créer une version intégrant les énergies renouvelables. Vous réalisez une affiche qui expose votre projet en insistant sur les intérêts qu'il présente pour la sauvegarde de la planète.

ACTIVITÉ LANGAGIÈRE	NIVEAU VISÉ
Expression écrite	**B1**

CAPACITÉS À METTRE EN ŒUVRE

⚙ Décrire un produit.

⚙ Présenter les avantages et inconvénients d'un produit.

⚙ Exposer des solutions et suggérer ou proposer des modifications.

⚙ Expliquer la mise en service et le fonctionnement d'appareils et de matériel.

⚙ Réaliser une affiche, un panneau.

Turn your face to the sun

 BOÎTE À OUTILS

Comparer	Le comparatif	The blue one's larger than the black one. And now my office is much more pleasant to work in.
	Le superlatif	Using solar power is the cheapest solution. That's the best news I've heard for a long time.
Exposer/ illustrer/ donner des exemples	Outils de présentation et d'organisation du propos	This is an advantage we can't deny. What I mean is that it is pretty urgent. Well, to begin with, I'd like to explain what happened exactly.
Donner son avis/ apprécier	L'expression de la subjectivité	I think… I don't like the idea of… In my opinion it makes a difference.
	La modalisation	Personally I believe we should carry on. We'd better change our habits.
	Adverbes	I quite like…
	Le superlatif	This is the greatest invention I've ever seen!
Démontrer/ justifier/ persuader	Articulations du discours	The reason is… The thing is… In order to reduce our energy consumption…
	Relations logiques (cause, conséquence, but)	Fresh water will be generated thanks to a solar power desalinating plant.

1

Cartoon

Origin: © Ben Heine, www.benheine.com

2

Renewable energy consumption in the US (2003-2007)

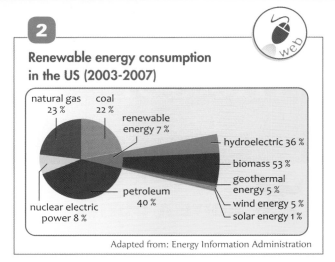

natural gas 23 %
coal 22 %
renewable energy 7 %
hydroelectric 36 %
biomass 53 %
geothermal energy 5 %
wind energy 5 %
solar energy 1 %
petroleum 40 %
nuclear electric power 8 %

Adapted from: Energy Information Administration

3

Renewable energies TV spot

4

Windfarm

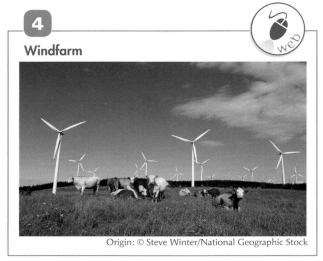

Origin: © Steve Winter/National Geographic Stock

5

Wind farms are a winner

If somebody had mentioned wind farms 70 years ago, it might have been considered a bad joke. In May 1934, one of the worst dust storms on record spread across the land from Montana and the Dakotas all the way to the Eastern Seaboard. [...]

Wind was associated with topsoil loss and crop disasters back then. Today, wind is more likely to be viewed by farmers as renewable energy. In fact, the states that spawned those dust storms rank high in wind energy potential today. [...]

The American Wind Energy Association has a vision of wind energy supplying 20 per cent of U.S. electricity needs by 2030. That's a big leap forward from the present, with wind just a sliver on a pie chart of electricity generation – less than 1 per cent. [...]

Most wind farms are on private land, typically agricultural land that is leased. There are a few developments on public lands in the West. [...]

Wind power's attraction is as an inexhaustible, nonpolluting source of energy that uses no water to produce electricity. It looks even more promising when stacked up against the leading fossil fuel alternatives, coal-fired generation and natural gas. [...]

Wind is a variable source of energy, but a new wind farm undergoes a one-year period of site testing before construction to make sure the location is suitable. Sloan says reaction to wind farms in rural areas is mostly positive. They produce local income, jobs and tax revenue in addition to electricity and make a contribution to what the public says it wants – clean, renewable forms of energy.

Origin: © 2010, American Farm Bureau Association

6

Scotland: environmentally friendly family wins award

A West Lothian family have won a £10,000 prize – thanks to their environmentally friendly endeavours. The McDermids from West Calder have won the National Sustainability Award and bursary that comes with it. They triumphed over tough competition to win the public vote in the prestigious Future Friendly Awards, receiving the prize of a home and eco makeover worth £10,000.

The Future Friendly Awards is a nationwide search for communities and families who are making a real difference by championing sustainability and environmentally friendly practices.

Judith McDermid, along with husband George and children Beth and Rory, have been taking small steps to lighten their impact on the environment since they moved into their home 14 years ago. Just one of the family's many steps included fully double glazing their home and adding a heat recovery ventilation system that takes heat from a south fa‑cing conservatory into the house. The family only use energy efficient lightbulbs and have a wood burning stove to keep their gas consumption down. In autumn last year they were able to live off their own land for two months, growing vege‑tables and eating eggs from the chickens that roam freely in their garden, along with collecting rainwater, recycling using compost and a wormery, only holidaying in the UK and doing all short journeys on foot or by bike. Every year they have a waste audit to see where they can cut down on waste and they monitor their fuel use on a weekly basis.

Origin: © West Lothian courier

7

Saving energy

8

Biofuel

Liquid biofuel is usually either bioalcohol such as bioethanol or an oil such as biodiesel.

Bioethanol is an alcohol made by fermenting the sugar components of plant materials and it is made mostly from sugar and starch crops. With advanced technology being developed, cellulosic biomass, such as trees and grasses, are also used as feedstocks for ethanol production. Ethanol can be used as a fuel for vehicles in its pure form, but it is usually used as a gasoline additive to increase octane and improve vehicle emissions. Bioethanol is widely used in the USA and in Brazil.

Biodiesel is made from vegetable oils, animal fats or recycled greases. Biodiesel can be used as a fuel for vehicles in its pure form, but it is usually used as a diesel additive to reduce levels of particulates, carbon monoxide, and hydrocarbons from diesel-powered vehicles. Biodiesel is produced from oils or fats using transesterification and is the most common biofuel in Europe.

Biofuels provided 1.8 % of the world's transport fuel in 2008.

Origin: cc by-sa Wikipedia, http://en.wikipedia.org/wiki/Renewable_energy

9

Ethanol petrol

Origin: cc by M. Côté

11

Solar power

10

Renewable energy debate

Renewable electricity production, from sources such as wind power and solar power, is sometimes criticized for being variable or intermittent. However, the International Energy Agency has stated that deployment of renewable technologies usually increases the diversity of electricity sources and, through local generation, contributes to the flexibility of the system and its resistance to central shocks.

There have been "not in my back yard" (NIMBY) concerns relating to the visual and other impacts of some wind farms, with local residents sometimes fighting or blocking construction. In the USA, the Massachusetts Cape Wind project was delayed for years partly because of aesthetic concerns. However, residents in other areas have been more positive and there are many examples of community wind farm developments. According to a town councilor, the overwhelming majority of locals believe that the Ardros‑san Wind Farm in Scotland has enhanced the area.

Origin: cc by-sa Wikipedia, http://en.wikipedia.org/wiki/Renewable_energy

12

Masdar: Abu Dhabi's carbon neutral city

The world's first zero-carbon city is being built in Abu Dhabi and is designed to be not only free of cars and skyscrapers but also powered by the sun.

The oil-rich United Arab Emirates is the last place you would expect to learn lessons on low-carbon living, but the emerging eco-city of Masdar could teach the world. [...]

The inhospitable terrain suggests that the only way to survive here is with the maximum of technological support, a bit like living on the moon. [...] Masdar will be home to about 50,000 people, at least 1,000 businesses and a university.

[...] It will cost between £10bn ($15bn) and £20bn ($30bn).

Renewable energy

The architects are turning the desert's greatest threat – the sun – into their greatest asset.

They have built the biggest solar farm in the Middle East to power the city and to offset the inevitable burning of diesel and baking of cement in construction.

They are also experimenting. One project involves a circular field of mirrors on the ground, all reflecting towards a tower in the middle.

That, in turn, bounces the light down in a concentrated beam about a metre (3ft) wide to produce heat and drive generators.

But I was told firmly not to wander over and feel the warmth, as it could fry me in seconds. [...]

Keeping cool

The Emirates have seen one of the world's most spectacular building booms paid for by oil and made tolerable by air conditioners, which also depend on oil to feed their vast appetite for energy.

But Masdar will have to be low temperature and low carbon.

Part of the solution is apparent the moment you walk in.

And you do "walk in" because this is a city surrounded by a wall, a defined boundary.

[...] Masdar is compact like ancient Arab cities.

Streets are narrow so buildings shade each other, and the walls and roofs of buildings will do their bit to shed heat too.

The vertical faces are dressed with screens which look like a terracotta mesh. They keep the sun out but let the breeze in.

And as architect Gerard Evenden says: "Lunar technology has begun to influence our thinking".

One idea being tested is using a thin foil surface covering, a gas or vacuum blanket, to keep the heat out. It is an idea dreamt up for a moon base.

To encourage a breeze, wind towers are being built, drawing draughts through the streets without using energy.

Masdar will still use electricity for gadgets, some air conditioning and, most crucially, to desalinate sea water but, when it comes to power, the city has a simple mantra: "Only use energy when you have exhausted design".

Driverless vehicles

Conventional cars must be checked in at the city gates and then you can choose between the oldest and newest modes of transport.

At street level, it is all pedestrianised and the planners have done their best to keep the city compact and foot-friendly.

But if fatigue overtakes you, then slip down a level and meet the Personal Rapid Transit or podcars.

These driverless vehicles are guided by magnetic sensors, powered by solar electricity, and they stop automatically if an obstacle appears. They are programmed to go where you ask.

By T. Heap - Sunday, 28 March 2010

Origin: © from BBC News at bbc.co.uk/news

13

Environmental phones

The growing number of mobile telephones no longer in use is causing problems for the environment. In response, a new phone has been developed, and it turns into a flower...

Disused mobile phones are becoming a serious danger for the environment. In Europe alone, over a hundred million phones are thrown away every year. Now, scientists at the UK's Warwick University have developed a creative solution: the biodegradable phone.

As *The Guardian* reports, the new phone will break down on the compost heap into a pile of soil nutrients. The scientists have even devised a way of embedding a plant seed into the phone cover. When the phone is thrown away, the seed will germinate into a flower.

D. Walter

Origin: © Bayard Presse/*Today in English*, April 2005

Environmentalists worried about the problem of disused mobile phones will be pleased to see biodegradable phones grow into flowers.

PISTES PÉDAGOGIQUES

doc. 1 Ce document iconographique introduit le thème de l'environnement, en partant du postulat que nous avons un choix à faire pour l'avenir de la planète. Deux visions et deux projets s'opposent. Le document amène les apprenants à réfléchir sur les enjeux de ce choix pour l'environnement et permet de faire l'évaluation diagnostique de l'état de leurs connaissances.

doc. 2 Ce diagramme centre la thématique sur les énergies renouvelables et situe la place qu'elles occupent dans notre consommation actuelle. Sa description permet de réutiliser le comparatif et le superlatif. L'enseignant peut ensuite demander aux apprenants de se projeter dans l'avenir et d'imaginer la place qu'occuperont demain les énergies renouvelables.

doc. 3 Ce document audio de la Commission européenne présente les énergies renouvelables. Il permet une acquisition lexicale significative. La vidéo intégrale de ce document est disponible sur le site compagnon.

doc. 4, 5 Cette photo (doc. 4) permet d'introduire le document sonore (doc. 5) qui explique que le vent, autrefois considéré comme une nuisance, est aujourd'hui un atout économique. Lors de la phase d'anticipation, les apprenants sont amenés à réfléchir sur les avantages et les inconvénients de l'éolien.

doc. 6 Ce texte est extrait d'un article sur une famille récompensée pour ses efforts en matière de respect de l'environnement. L'enseignant demande aux apprenants de relever les exemples concrets de pratiques respectueuses de l'environnement citées dans le texte, et ensuite de les comparer avec leur propre vécu.

doc. 7, 8, 9 Ces documents illustrent l'utilisation des énergies renouvelables dans le secteur de l'automobile. Le document 9 peut être l'occasion de travailler la voie passive : on peut, par exemple, demander aux apprenants de faire des recherches et d'expliquer les différentes étapes de fabrication de l'éthanol.

doc. 10 Cet article démontre que les énergies renouvelables ne font pas l'unanimité. À partir des arguments développés dans cet article et des connaissances acquises à travers l'étude des documents précédents, les apprenants sont en mesure de produire une synthèse des avantages et inconvénients des énergies renouvelables.

doc. 11 Ce document audio peut, dans une phase d'anticipation, permettre aux apprenants de réfléchir sur les utilisations possibles de l'énergie solaire au quotidien. L'étude du document doit permettre de compléter la liste produite par les apprenants et fournir un lexique pour la réalisation de la tâche finale.

doc. 12 À partir de cet article sur un projet de construction aux Émirats arabes unis de la première ville 100 % écologique, les apprenants listent les innovations, en expliquant leur fonctionnement et leurs avantages. On peut également leur demander de dessiner, à partir des informations données dans le texte, un plan de la ville et de présenter leur travail à l'oral.

doc. 13 Cet article présente une version recyclable du téléphone portable. On peut demander aux apprenants de se positionner sur le contenu de l'article (« Croyez-vous cela possible ? Pourquoi ? »). Les apprenants peuvent s'inspirer de l'exemple décrit dans cet article pour réaliser la tâche finale.

TÂCHE FINALE

En s'appuyant sur l'exemple du téléphone portable présenté dans le document 13, les apprenants choisissent un objet familier dont ils imaginent une version intégrant une ou des énergie(s) renouvelable(s). Ils réalisent individuellement une affiche, qui doit comporter la description de l'objet, avant et après transformation, et mettent en avant les avantages du projet pour l'environnement.

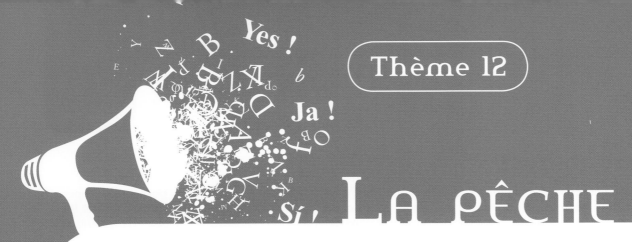

LA PÊCHE

TÂCHE FINALE

Vous présentez à votre voisin étranger votre projet militant d'installation de pisciculture comme alternative à la surpêche des océans.

ACTIVITÉ LANGAGIÈRE	NIVEAU VISÉ
Expression orale en continu et en interaction	**B1**

CAPACITÉS À METTRE EN ŒUVRE

⚙ Présenter un projet.

⚙ Décrire simplement des travaux à réaliser.

⚙ Fournir un éclaircissement.

⚙ Justifier un choix.

⚙ Réagir à des objections.

⚙ S'assurer que son interlocuteur a compris les informations transmises.

Take care of the Earth and she will take care of you

BOÎTE À OUTILS

Nommer/ désigner	Le singulier et le pluriel	His name's… / Their names are…
	La détermination	This is a… John is the man who runs the fishery.
	Outils de la localisation spatiale	It's there. Where? Right here, on your left!
	Adjectifs et pronoms démonstratifs	This is what I plan to do. This is it! I don't like those.
	Le génitif	The fishermen's nets. A fishmonger's responsibility. His neighbour's project is based on sustainability. This is Peter's office.
Qualifier	Adjectifs épithètes et attributs	The fish smells good. It's got omega 3 fats.
	Adverbes	She really cares for sustainable fishing. Seafood is always contaminated. We'll never buy endangered species.
	Mots composés	Farm-raised species. Deep-frying can seal in toxins.
Quantifier	Le singulier et le pluriel	I need two boats, not one. He's only thirty-five.
	Adjectifs cardinaux	I got two hundred pounds for it. It cost over three hundred pounds.
	Quantificateurs	How much does it cost? How many tons do you plan to produce? Ten? They gave us very little information. Several of these endangered species… Give me half of it. I sold it for one third of the regular price.

1

A cartoon by Stan Eales

Origin: © www.CartoonStock.com

2

Sustainable fishing

Our solutions: sustainable fishing [...]

Mackerel caught according to the standard of Marine Stewardship Council (MSC), UK.

What's the problem?

Unsustainable fishing – caused by poor fisheries management and wasteful, destructive fishing practices – is decimating the world's fisheries, as well as destroying marine habitats and killing billions of unwanted fish and other marine animals each year.

As a result, the future of the fishing industry is under threat – as are already endangered marine species and habitats, and the livelihoods and food security of millions of people.

Origin: © WWF, http://wwf.panda.org/what_we_do/how_we_work/conservation/marine/sustainable_fishing/

3

Sustainable seafood

Around the world, many traditional fisheries are threatened with collapse, due to unsustainable fishing practices and habitat destruction.

Some fisheries, however, remain healthy and productive due to successful management, responsible harvesting and advances in contained fish farming.

Tips

– Try to choose shellfish grown on farms using racks, lines or nets which are suspended in the water. These methods minimize damage to bottom habitat during harvesting.

– Striped bass, a well-managed Atlantic coast species, can be used as a substitute for some depleted species, such as black sea bass, rock cod, red snapper, grouper and roughy.

– Farmed crawfish make an excellent substitute for lobster, which, although plentiful are often harvested at minimum size – before having a chance at reproduction.

– Sea foods can be contaminated with mercury, PCB's and other pollutants. Contaminants are mostly stored in fatty tissue, so grilling and broiling when cooking fish is recommended to allow fats and juices to drain away. Deep-frying can seal in toxins which may be stored in fat. In general, cooking fish, as opposed to eating it raw, can reduce contaminant levels by about 30 %.

– Ask your local seafood dealer or restaurateur about the source and catch-method of your seafood choices. Consumer concern is the best promoter of sustainable fisheries.

Origin: Eartheasy.com © 2001-2010

4

Overfishing

Overfishing occurs when fishing activities reduce fish stocks below an acceptable level. This can occur in any body of water from a pond to the oceans. [...]

Types of overfishing

There are three recognized types of overfishing: growth overfishing, recruit overfishing and ecosystem overfishing.

Growth overfishing – is when fish are harvested at an average size that is smaller than the size that would produce the maximum yield per recruit. This makes the total yield less than it would be if the fish were allowed to grow to a reasonable size. [...]

Recruit overfishing – is when the mature adult (spawning biomass) population is depleted to a level where it no longer has the reproductive capacity to replenish itself. There are not enough adults to produce offspring. [...]

Ecosystem overfishing – is when the balance of the ecosystem is altered due to overfishing. The abundances of large predatory species decline and in turn small forage type species increase in abundance, causing a shift in the balance of the ecosystem towards smaller species of fish.

Origin: cc by-sa Wikipedia, http://en.wikipedia.org/wiki/Overfishing

Take care of the Earth and she will take care of you

5

A photograph taken in the Gulf of Maine, USA

Origin: © Bill Curtsinger/National Geographic Stock

6

Ocean Fisheries Recovering

7

Lundy

Lundy is the largest island in the Bristol Channel, lying 12 miles (19 km) off the coast of Devon, England, approximately one third of the distance across the channel between England and Wales. [...]

As of 2007, there was a resident population of 28 people, including volunteers. These include a warden, island manager, and farmer, as well as bar and house-keeping staff. Most live in and around the village at the south of the island. Most visitors are day-trippers, although there are 23 holiday properties and a camp site for staying visitors, mostly also around the south of the island.

In a 2005 opinion poll of *Radio Times* readers, Lundy was named as Britain's tenth greatest natural wonder. The entire island has been designated as a Site of Special Scientific Interest and it was England's first statutory Marine Nature Reserve, and the first Marine Conservation Zone, because of its unique flora and fauna. It is managed by the Landmark Trust on behalf of the National Trust.

Origin: cc by-sa Wikipedia, http://en.wikipedia.org/wiki/Lundy

8

Learning how to farm fish

FAO's aquaculture training helps rural development

Rep Hing knows 24 different ways of preparing fish. She grills, fries, salts, steams and ferments them. Luckily, both she and her family of 25 like fish. They eat fish almost every day, raising them right behind their house in the Siem Reap province in northern Cambodia.

Two years ago Ms Rep participated in an FAO aquaculture training course. "We learned how to build and repair a fish pond, how to raise fingerlings and how to produce the feed for the fish", said Ms Rep, who today has two fish ponds with five different kinds of fish. She has also received training in farming fish in her rice fields and raising fingerlings. "It is not difficult to farm fish and it is good for our family", she said. "We eat better and we also earn money". [...]

Aquaculture is an important contributor to poverty alleviation, food security and social well-being in many countries like Cambodia. Approximately 90 per cent of global production comes from developing countries, and a large proportion of this comes from small-scale producers such as Ms Rep. [...]

Aquaculture contributes almost a third of global fisheries landings. Today fish represents 15.9 percent of the total animal protein supply worldwide, higher than all other meat products. People living in Asia and Africa are much more dependent on fish as part of their daily diets than are people living in other regions of the world. An example is the Philippines, where more than 50 per cent of the protein intake comes from fish.

Origin: © Food and Agriculture Organization of th United Nations

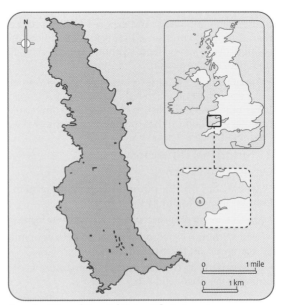

Lundy: Site of Special Scientific Interest

9

Sustainable backyard fishery

Research team trumpets sustainable backyard fishery

A research team at Vancouver Island University's School of Fisheries and Aquaculture has developed an innovative aquaponic system where fish are used to fertilize vegetables and vice versa.

The system works by using food waste produced by the fish to feed vegetables, which in turn filter the water for the fish.

Origin: © Used with the permission of CBC News

11

Wild vs Farmed fish

Is there any nutritional difference between wild-caught and farm-raised fish? Is one type better for me than the other?

1 - Overview

From both a nutritional and environmental impact perspective, farmed fish are far inferior to their wild counterparts:

• Despite being much fattier, farmed fish provide less usable beneficial omega 3 fats than wild fish.

• Due to the feedlot conditions of aquafarming, farm-raised fish are doused with antibiotics and exposed to more concentrated pesticides than their wild kin. Farmed salmon, in addition, are given a salmon-colored dye in their feed, without which, their flesh would be an unappetizing grey color.

• Aquafarming also raises a number of environmental concerns, the most important of which may be its negative impact on wild salmon. It has now been established that sea lice from farms kill up to 95 % of juvenile wild salmon that migrate past them. (Krkosek M, Lewis MA., Proc. Natl. Acad. Sci. USA)

2 - Nutritional Differences

Omega 3 Fat Content

FDA statistics on the nutritional content (protein and fat-ratios) of farm versus wild salmon show that:

• The fat content of farmed salmon is excessively high — 30-35 % by weight.

• Wild salmon have a 20 % higher protein content and a 20 % lower fat content than farm-raised salmon.

• Farm-raised fish contain much higher amounts of pro-inflammatory omega 6 fats than wild fish.

Origin: © 2001-2010 The George Mateljan Foundation

10

Electrofishing

What is an electrofishing survey?

An electrofishing survey is one of the most effective lake management and pond management tools available today. With the proper equipment, we are able to take fish samples from your pond or lake. In this process, we will be able to determine, stocking densities, health & proportion of fish, and detect disease or worm infestations. Once the survey is completed all fish are returned to your pond or lake. After the survey, you will receive an assessment and recommendations. This will give you the insight you need to make informed decisions in the management of your pond or lake.

How does it work?

Electricity is passed through the water, by two types of electrodes, the anode (positive) and the cathode (negative). When applying the correct current, fish will experience a muscle response reaction called taxis. This will cause a swimming motion toward the anode. Once the fish reaches the anode, swimming will stop. The fish will go into a state of narcosis (stunned). Narcosis will only last for a few seconds. At this point, the fish are netted and put into a holding tank for observation. After observation, the fish are released.

Origin: © Dunn's Fish Farms, www.dunnsfishfarm.com

12

Maldive tuna fishing

Take care of the Earth and she will take care of you

PISTES PÉDAGOGIQUES

doc. 1, 2, 3   Le dessin humoristique (doc. 1) ainsi que les deux textes qui le suivent (doc. 2 et 3) permettent une introduction simple à un problème complexe, celui de la surpêche. Le choix de la « moissonneuse-pêcheuse » dans le premier document permet d'attirer l'attention des apprenants les moins sensibilisés au problème de la pêche intensive. En complément, le document 2 présente de manière dense mais linguistiquement accessible les données du problème, qui doivent être comprises pour maintenir l'intérêt des apprenants jusqu'à la production de la tâche finale. Le document 3 illustre le document 2 au travers d'exemples et de conseils précis. Sa compréhension détaillée, indispensable, ne peut se faire que grâce à une aide lexicale significative.

doc. 4   Cet article présente une approche plus théorique de la surpêche. La compréhension de ce document doit être détaillée et nécessite une aide soutenue de la part de l'enseignant. La richesse du lexique doit permettre de fournir aux apprenants de nombreux outils linguistiques utiles à la réalisation de la tâche finale.

doc. 5   Cette photo permet, si l'enseignant le souhaite, de réactiver le champ lexical de la surpêche mais elle doit avant tout être utilisée comme support à l'activité de pré-écoute du document 6. L'enseignant doit veiller à ce que la formulation d'hypothèses s'oriente sur les zones de pêche de la planète et les problèmes qui persistent.

doc. 6   Ce document audio propose un état des lieux de la pêche. Si le titre peut faire penser à une amélioration de la situation, l'étude détaillée de ce document montre que l'Europe doit faire face au problème de la surpêche. Une mini-tâche peut servir d'objectif de compréhension : sur un planisphère simplifié, on peut demander aux apprenants de colorier les noms de lieux en fonction de l'état de la pêche dans les zones mentionnées.

doc. 7   Ce texte apporte un regard complémentaire sur le problème de la surpêche. Facilement accessible aux apprenants, sa compréhension peut servir d'introduction à une tâche intermédiaire qui consiste à faire s'exprimer la classe sur ce que peut être le *Special Scientific Interest* de ce site, comme l'indique la légende de la carte.

doc. 8, 9, 10, 11   Cet ensemble constitue une base pour l'étude de la pêche d'élevage. Selon l'intérêt de la classe, la totalité des documents peut être étudiée par tous les apprenants ; on peut aussi envisager une étude par groupe, conduisant à une tâche intermédiaire qui consiste à rapporter oralement, devant le groupe ou la classe, les informations présentant un intérêt pour l'exécution de la tâche finale.

doc. 12   Cette vidéo présente des images fortes. Son exploitation pédagogique peut se faire à différents stades de l'étude du thème. Elle peut être visionnée après l'étude des documents sur la surpêche et la pêche durable afin de montrer qu'il existe des alternatives, ou à la fin de l'étude du thème, pour permettre une réactivation langagière de certains des aspects étudiés.

TÂCHE FINALE

On doit privilégier, dans un souci d'authenticité, le travail en binôme ou en groupe, présenté oralement devant une partie des apprenants. Des grilles d'observation et de co-évaluation sont disponibles sur de nombreux sites pédagogiques sur Internet, ou peuvent être créées par l'enseignant.

ANIMATION DE L'ESPACE RURAL, SERVICE EN MILIEU RURAL

COMMERCIALISATION DE PRODUITS AGRICOLES

TÂCHE FINALE

C'est le début des vacances et de nombreux touristes étrangers viennent d'arriver dans votre région. Vous avez été contacté(e) par l'office de tourisme pour intervenir dans les campings afin de leur présenter les différentes productions agricoles locales et leurs points de vente (marchés, foires, vente directe chez le producteur). Après avoir fait des recherches sur Internet ou à l'office de tourisme, vous réalisez une brochure en anglais, que vous présentez et distribuez lors d'une soirée de présentation au camping. Vous répondez ensuite aux différentes questions et observations des touristes.

ACTIVITÉ LANGAGIÈRE	NIVEAU VISÉ
Expression écrite et expression orale en continu et en interaction	**B1**

CAPACITÉS À METTRE EN ŒUVRE

⚙ Réaliser un dépliant publicitaire.

⚙ Décrire un lieu, des personnes.

⚙ Décrire un produit.

⚙ Décrire une activité professionnelle.

⚙ Présenter les avantages d'un produit.

⚙ Répondre à des demandes de renseignements.

... sell like hot cake

 BOÎTE À OUTILS

Nommer/ désigner	La détermination	John is the man who runs the farm.
	Adjectifs démonstratifs	This market is…
	Outils de la localisation spatiale	It's there, on your left.
Qualifier	Adjectifs épithètes et attributs	The fruits are organic.
	Adverbes	Food is really extraordinary. The farmer always gives you the best.
	Mots composés	It's a three-star farm.
Comparer	Le comparatif	Arlington market is bigger than Durham's.
	Le superlatif	The best cheese-maker.
Situer dans l'espace	Compléments, prépositions et adverbes de lieu	On your right… / Up the hill… It's two miles away.
Donner des indications	Adverbes et locutions de temps, de lieu	When you arrive, drop in for a visit.
Démontrer/ justifier/ persuader	Articulations du discours	The reason is… The thing is… They organise a tour of the plant so that you see how they work.
	Relations logiques (cause, conséquence, but)	Thanks to a new workshop, they can produce more.

1

Supermarket

Origin: © K. Corvellec

2

Shop locally

Origin: © www.CartoonStock.com

3

What is a farmers' market?

Farmers' markets, sometimes called greenmarkets and green grocers, are markets, usually held outdoors, in public spaces, where farmers can sell produce to the public. Whereas these markets were commonplace before the Industrial age, they were often replaced in modernized cities with grocery stores that sell food that is usually pre-packaged and shipped from long distances.

[...]

Farmers' market produce is renowned for being locally grown and very fresh. People argue farmers' markets allow farmers to pick produce at the peak of flavor, preserve the nutritional content of fresh produce, and since locally grown produce does not travel as far to get to your table, the difference in mileage saves fossil fuels.

Farmers' markets often feature produce grown naturally or organically, meats that are raised humanely on pasture, handmade farmstead cheeses, eggs and poultry from free-range fowl, as well as heirloom produce and heritage breeds of meat and fowl. In many countries with strict food safety laws, farmers' markets can be one of the few places beyond the farm gate to purchase raw food, such as raw milk.

Farmers' market advocates believe the markets help farmers stay in business as well as preserve natural resources.

Wholesale prices farmers get for their produce are very low, often near the cost of production. Farmers who sell direct to the public without going through a middle man get a better price. It can be shown that the preservation of farmland is important for the health of the environment and water supply. According to the American Farmland Trust, sustainable and managed farms conserve soil and clean water and provide a habitat for wildlife. Moreover, modern farmers' markets help maintain important social ties, linking rural and urban populations and even close neighbors in mutually rewarding exchange.

Farmers' markets are a traditional way of selling agricultural and home manufactured products. A weekly market day is a part of normal life in villages and town squares throughout the world.

Origin: cc by-sa Wikipedia,
http://en.wikipedia.org/wiki/
Farmers%27_market

... sell like hot cake

4

Number of operating farmers' markets

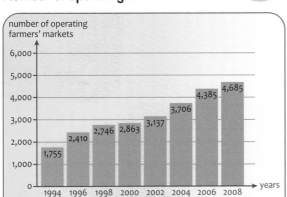

number of operating farmers' markets

Year	Markets
1994	1,755
1996	2,410
1998	2,746
2000	2,863
2002	3,137
2004	3,706
2006	4,385
2008	4,685

average increase: 6.8 %

Adapted from: USDA-AMS-Marketing Service Division

5

Farmers' markets vs supermarkets

Growing up in the San Joaquin Valley of California, considered to be the "agricultural center of the world", I am familiar with farmers' markets. My grandfather sold oranges at a roadside market once a year. I appreciate the fact that farmers' markets provide local, quality produce, however, I must confess that until doing research for this article I thought of the prices of produce at farmers' markets as being much more expensive than supermarkets.

In a study of California farmers' markets, titled "California Farmers Markets Price Perceptions", 54 per cent of sellers at California farmers' markets "actually charged lower prices than supermarkets on a cumulative 345 items". Another 44 per cent said they set prices equivalent to supermarkets on a "a cumulative 259 produce items". [...]

"There's sort of a common perception that the farmers' market is more expensive. A lot of people feel they're doing the farmers a favor".

Gina-Mary Cheeseman

Origin: © Celsias, www.celsias.com

6

Why do people go to farmers' markets?

You go to the market because there is so much going on. The up side is that you feel refreshed by markets that are basically entertainment venues. The down side is that it takes a lot of money and energy for advertising, marketing and the other components of the modern corporate business model that focuses on growth.

Farmers markets in this country are quite different from those I have seen in Mexico, Guatemala, El Salvador, Britain, Norway, and Italy. In those countries the markets serve as places to buy food and other items that are necessary for life. There may be some entertainment, but the focus is NOT on getting the customer to "feel good". It is simply to provide a place for farmers and other small-scale businesspeople to sell their products. These markets operate at low cost to the vendor and the city in which they are located.

Farmers markets in this country have missed the boat. By focusing on the entertainment venue model, they have locked themselves into high costs and thus must charge high stall fees. [...]

It is not the case that the customer is demanding the entertainment venue style of farmers market. The customer is not given the other alternative.

Origin: © 2010, LocalHarvest

7

Slow food

Slow Food is an international movement founded by Carlo Petrini in 1986. Promoted as an alternative to fast food, it strives to preserve traditional and regional cuisine and encourages farming of plants, seeds and livestock characteristic of the local ecosystem. It was the first established part of the broader Slow movement. The movement has since expanded globally to over 100,000 members in 132 countries. Its goals of sustainable foods and promotion of local small businesses are paralleled by a political agenda directed against globalization of agricultural products.

Origin: cc by-sa Wikipedia, http://en.wikipedia.org/wiki/Slow_food

8

CSA: Community Supported Agriculture

Thinking about signing up for a CSA but want to learn more about the idea before you commit? Read on.

Over the last 20 years, Community Supported Agriculture (CSA) has become a popular way for consumers to buy local, seasonal food directly from a farmer. Here are the basics: a farmer offers a certain number of "shares" to the public. Typically the share consists of a box of vegetables, but other farm products may be included. Interested consumers purchase a share (aka a "membership" or a "subscription") and in return receive a box (bag, basket) of seasonal produce each week throughout the farming season.

This arrangement creates several rewards for both the farmer and the consumer. In brief...

Advantages for farmers:

Get to spend time marketing the food early in the year, before their 16 hour days in the field begin.

Receive payment early in the season, which helps with the farm's cash flow.

Have an opportunity to get to know the people who eat the food they grow.

Advantages for consumers:

Eat ultra-fresh food, with all the flavor and vitamin benefits.

Get exposed to new vegetables and new ways of cooking.

Usually get to visit the farm at least once a season.

Find that kids typically favor food from "their" farm — even veggies they've never been known to eat.

Develop a relationship with the farmer who grows their food and learn more about how food is grown.

Origin: © 2010 LocalHarvest

9

New laws in US claim to increase food safety

10

Farm-to-table movement

Farm-to-table (or farm-to-fork) refers to, in the food safety field, the stages of the production of food: harvesting, storage, processing, packaging, sales, and consumption. Farm-to-table also refers to a movement concerned with producing food locally and delivering that food to local consumers. [...]

Many farm-to-table advocates cite the works of [...] Joel Salatin and others in their preference for the freshest ingredients and in their attempts to educate their customers about the link between farmers, farm communities, ancient food-production practices, and the food we eat. [...]

Farm-to-table restaurants may buy their produce directly from farmers, usually local. In a few cases, the res-taurants and farms may be owned and operated by the same people. The farm-to-table movement has arisen more or less concurrently with recent changes in attitude about food safety, food freshness, food seasonality, and small-farm economics. Advocates and practitioners of the farm-to-table model frequently cite as their motivations the scarcity of fresh, local ingredients; the poor flavor of ingredients shipped from afar; the poor nutritional integrity of shipped ingredients; the encroachment of genetically modified foods into the food economy; the disappearance of small family farms; the disappearance of heirloom and open-pollinated fruits and vegetables; and the dangers of a highly-centralized food-growing and distribution system.

Origin: cc by-sa Wikipedia, http://en.wikipedia.org/wiki/Farm_to_fork

PISTES PÉDAGOGIQUES

doc. 1, 2 Ces deux documents iconographiques ont pour rôle de contextualiser le sujet et de faire l'état des lieux des connaissances des apprenants. Deux systèmes de commercialisation des produits agricoles sont présentés ici. Les apprenants comparent les deux systèmes en fonction de leur expérience personnelle.

doc. 3 Ce texte propose une définition de ce qu'est un *farmers' market* et permet d'acquérir le lexique nécessaire à la réalisation de la tâche finale.

doc. 4 Ce graphique présente l'évolution du nombre de *farmers'markets* aux États-Unis. Il s'agit ici de recentrer le sujet sur une analyse factuelle afin que l'apprenant prenne connaissance de la situation avant d'exprimer une opinion personnelle. Les apprenants sont invités à émettre des hypothèses sur les raisons de cette évolution (« La situation est-elle similaire en France ? Qu'est-ce que cela révèle sur les consommateurs ?... »).

doc. 5 Ce texte établit une comparaison entre les prix des produits agricoles vendus sur les marchés et ceux de la grande distribution. Comme la question du prix des produits a préalablement été abordée lors de l'étude des documents précédents, ce document permet d'apporter des arguments supplémentaires dans le débat. La dernière phrase du texte amène les apprenants à réfléchir sur les critères de choix des consommateurs.
TÂCHE INTERMÉDIAIRE POSSIBLE : lister quelques produits et réaliser une étude comparative de leur prix en grande distribution et sur les marchés environnants.

doc. 6 Cet extrait d'un fil de discussions offre un point de vue plus contrasté sur les raisons pour lesquelles les consommateurs choisissent d'acheter leurs produits sur les marchés.
TÂCHE INTERMÉDIAIRE POSSIBLE : à partir des documents 4 et 5, et des hypothèses émises par les apprenants, réaliser un questionnaire listant les différentes motivations qui poussent les personnes à acheter certains produits (« Quels produits ? ») au marché. En faire une synthèse à l'oral devant la classe.

doc. 7 Cet article présente un nouveau mouvement appelé *Slow food*. Un travail de réflexion sur le nom et le logo du mouvement peut permettre d'anticiper la lecture de ce court texte, qui peut être l'occasion d'un travail de recherche sur les différents mouvements de consommation locale (noms, points communs et différences).

doc. 8 Ce texte présente un autre mode de commercialisation des produits agricoles, connu en France sous l'appellation AMAP (Association pour le maintien d'une agriculture paysanne). Cette alternative au supermarché et au marché offre des intérêts tant pour le consommateur que pour le producteur, que les apprenants doivent lister afin de pouvoir les comparer avec les autres formes de commercialisation étudiées précédemment.

doc. 9, 10 Ce document sonore (doc. 9) apporte des informations sur la législation en matière de commercialisation des produits agricoles aux États-Unis. Il peut être l'occasion de travailler sur les avantages et les inconvénients d'une législation en matière de sécurité alimentaire, tandis que le texte (doc. 10) présente une autre manière de concevoir la notion de fraîcheur des aliments, au travers du mouvement *Farm-to-table*.

TÂCHE FINALE

La tâche finale s'effectue en deux temps. Le travail de recherche et de réalisation du dépliant peut être réalisé en petits groupes. La présentation orale (individuelle) prend appui sur ce document que les apprenants présentent de manière dynamique (utilisation de dessins, d'images, de tableaux) au reste de la classe.

MAINTIEN DU MONDE RURAL

TÂCHE FINALE

Vous réalisez un sondage ou une interview auprès de la communauté anglophone de votre village afin de déterminer leurs besoins ou leurs attentes en matière de services de proximité.

ACTIVITÉ LANGAGIÈRE	NIVEAU VISÉ
Expression orale en interaction	**B1**

CAPACITÉS À METTRE EN ŒUVRE

⚙ Se présenter, établir un contact social.

⚙ Répondre à des demandes de renseignement.

⚙ Demander ou donner des descriptions, explications, informations sur des lieux, des événements, des institutions.

⚙ Partager ses idées, sentiments, émotions.

Country life...

 **BOÎTE À OUTILS**

Interroger	La syntaxe et l'intonation des énoncés interrogatifs	Do you think that...? What is your opinion on...? Where is the nearest petrol station? Can you repeat, please?
	Mots interrogatifs	Who / What / Where / When / Which / Who / Why / How...
Répondre	Énoncés elliptiques	I don't think so. Yes, sure! Yes, of course!
Maintenir/ relancer le dialogue	Gap fillers	Well / Err / Hum / I mean / Well, you see... / How shall I put it...
	Echoed questions	Oh, really? How's that?
Comparer	Comparatifs, superlatifs	It would be much more convenient to take the bus. Going by bus would be the quickest.
Donner son avis/ conseiller/ apprécier	L'expression de la subjectivité	To my mind / In my view / It seems to me that / What I think is.
	La modalisation	Personally I believe the government should do something about it. It might be a good idea to start a neighbourhood watch.

1

Windmill march

Origin: cc by A. Hay

2

The work of Rural Community Council

ACRE is the national umbrella body for Rural Community Councils across England. Together we are known as the Rural Community Action Network or RCAN.

Rural Community Councils work with rural communities, groups and individuals to develop projects, initiatives and approaches in response to this social change. The aim is to support sustainability ensuring that rural communities do not become a place where only the rich can afford to live.

Across the Rural Community Action Network there are specialist advisers to provide advice and support for a range of rural services. These services include:

– Transport;
– Community services – shops, post offices, health and social care;
– Young people;
– Childcare;
– Housing;
– Local area development and environmental improvements;
– Crime & community safety.

Origin: © ACRE

3

Rural services

   **And now...**

Services are the basis for any community – access to shops and post offices, healthcare, activities – create and enhance a feeling of belonging and a sustainable future for the area.

Rural communities have experienced significant social change over the last couple of decades. Very often villages do not offer adequate services for the local community to access, which forces people to travel out of their community to access services such as doctors' surgeries, schools, shops and post offices. For many, private transport, either a car or taxi, is the only way of accessing these services. The increased costs of accessing services together with the increased costs of housing has led to rural living becoming less and less affordable, and for some completely unaffordable. This is particularly a problem for older people, families with young children and young people.

[...]

Government and local authorities should provide a focus for the needs of rural services to help prevent closure and, where this happens, encourage solutions to support new ventures in rural areas through, for example, the planning system, grants and other support such as the provision of expertise and information. There must also be improved access to rural services through the provision of affordable transport solutions. If this does not happen, it is likely that rural communities will decline and there will be continued high car use.

Origin: © ACRE

4

Key facts

• Rural England has lost one fifth of its entire post office network since 2000.
• With more than 600 filling stations closing a year, motorists in some rural areas are being left up to 30 miles away from their nearest forecourt.
• Studies confirm that healthcare services cost more to provide in rural areas. It has been calculated that additional costs of between 7.5 per cent and 10 per cent are required to deliver health services to rural populations.
• People living in rural areas travel around 10,000 miles per year to access essential services – that's 43 per cent more than residents of towns.

Origin: © Countryside Alliance

5

Key services disappearing from rural England

Rural England in danger

Is village life in terminal decline? Well... it could be, according to a poll commissionned by the National Housing Federation.

Half the people interviewed say that access to key services has become a real challenge in recent years. Indeed, the figures speak for themselves: 2009 saw the closure of 650 pubs in rural areas! During the same period, at least 400 shops and 12 schools also disappeared from the rural landscape.

But the main problem seems to be the shortage of affordable homes in rural areas. "Prices have been pushed up by the arrival of wealthy second home owners" said the NHF executive Mr Orr. "There's a real danger that traditional life will disappear if local authorities don't draw up action plans to deliver the new homes so desperately needed".

Adapted from: www.politics.co.uk

6

An insight into rural England

8

The future for rural UK?

Hi,

I live in a fairly rural village location about 2 miles from the local telephone exchange. We currently receive broadband from BT at around 1.4 Mbs. What do you think the future will be for rural locations? Are we ever likely to get "superfast" broadband or fibre optic? Or is this just not cost effective?

PhilT1808, forum member

Origin: www.digitalspy.co.uk/PhilT1808

7

Computerization of villages

Origin: © www.CartoonStock.com

9

Broadband and rural communities

Need of high-speed broadband for rural communities

New rural community group made up of six national organizations has demanded for fast, reliable broadband services to meet the needs of rural communities. [...] Despite the government's proposals to bring minimum 2Mbps broadband to everyone in UK by 2012, 2 million people in rural areas do not get this speed, some get even less than 512Kbps. There are around 166,000 people living in rural and remote areas without any mode of broadband access, according to the Commission for Rural Communities.

Rural communities are left behind, when it comes to superfast broadband access as major broadband providers in UK do not consider remote areas for their investments. Rural homes as well as businesses in remote areas just do not get the benefits of high-speed broadband services, it was stated.

According to Charles Trotman, head of rural business development at the Country Land and Business Association, more than 100,000 small businesses in rural areas do not get broadband that can meet their needs. [...]

Earlier, Prince Charles wrote in the *Daily Telegraph* that many rural businesses, schools, doctors' surgeries and local authorities are just unable to cope with the slower Internet connection speeds. He also stressed the need of boosting rural economies with new investments.

10.12.2009

Origin: © 2009-2010 Broadband Analyst UK, www.broadbandanalyst.co.uk

10

Last post for rural post office?

Plans are afoot to close 2,500 post offices nationwide. The post office in the village of Burton Fleming in East Yorkshire is one of those facing closure. How would its closure affect local people?

Godfrey Coleman is the oldest person in the village of Burton Fleming.

[...] He says the post office has been an essential part of life for as long as he can recall - as well as offering the usual services, it fulfils a vital social role.

Everyone knows each other and staff at the post office [...]. If a resident does not visit at their usual time, the staff raise the alarm and other residents check on that person.

It's also a meeting place in Burton Fleming. With no pub and only a village hall, the post office is often the place for a chat. [...] If the post office closes, Godfrey will need to rely on the kindness of neighbours; he feels upset to think that means he will become dependent. [...]

And it's not just the elderly who fear the closure will change village life.

In such a cut-off area teenagers, especially, worry they will be more isolated than ever.

Sixteen-year-old Philip Wells [...] fears that if it closes the heart of the community will go with it.

"For younger people, well, there will be nothing," he warns. [...]

The government says just 4,000 post offices make money and that more than 80% of the rural network is not profitable.

Burton Fleming will find out on Monday if the village is to lose what it sees as a vital feature of its community.

By C. Marston

01.25.2008

Origin: from BBC News at bbc.co.uk/news

Country life...

PISTES PÉDAGOGIQUES

doc. 1   Cette photographie, prise lors de la campagne de 2007 contre la fermeture massive de bureaux de poste au Royaume-Uni, est une introduction au thème étudié. Elle doit amener les apprenants à dégager la problématique de l'accès aux services de proximité dans les zones rurales. Ce document peut également permettre d'anticiper le contenu du document 10.

doc. 2   Ce premier texte permet de sensibiliser les apprenants au rôle des associations militant pour la défense des services de proximité en milieu rural. La liste de ces services, qui figure en fin de document, peut servir de base à la réalisation d'une fiche d'aide à la lecture des documents 3, 4 et 5 (doc. 2bis et doc. 2ter).

doc. 3, 4, 5   Ces trois textes, riches en exemples et en données chiffrées, sont une illustration de la dégradation des services de proximité en zones rurales. On peut envisager une étude de ces documents par groupes, à l'aide de la fiche de compréhension réalisée précédemment, et procéder devant la classe à une restitution orale des informations relevées dans chaque document.

doc. 6   Ce témoignage audio peut être utilisé en complément des documents 3, 4 et 5. Son exploitation permet la réactivation du lexique vu précédemment. La vidéo intégrale de ce document est aussi disponible sur le site compagnon.

doc. 7, 8, 9   Ces trois documents abordent le problème de la fracture numérique entre zones urbaines et zones rurales. Les deux premiers documents permettent d'introduire cette problématique et d'anticiper la lecture du texte du document 9. Ce dernier document doit conduire les apprenants à relever des arguments mettant en avant les problèmes posés par l'absence de connexion Internet en haut débit dans certaines zones rurales.

doc. 10   Ce texte, qui fait écho à la photographie proposée en introduction (doc.1), met l'accent sur le rôle social du bureau de poste au sein d'un village. L'exploitation de ce document riche en vocabulaire nécessite un guidage précis de la part de l'enseignant. L'étude peut être précédée d'une phase d'anticipation consistant à répondre à la question exprimée dans le premier paragraphe : *How would its closure affect local people?*

TÂCHE FINALE

La réalisation de la tâche requiert un temps important de préparation au cours duquel les apprenants travaillent par groupes de quatre.

Un premier sous-groupe de deux apprenants joue le rôle des interviewers et prépare un ensemble de questions en s'appuyant sur les informations recueillies au travers des documents étudiés précédemment. Le deuxième sous-groupe endosse le rôle des membres de la communauté anglophone interrogés et commence par travailler sur les améliorations susceptibles d'être apportées aux services disponibles dans le village (transports, magasins, santé).

Le sondage ou l'interview qui suit peut durer de cinq à dix minutes.

SAUVEGARDE DU PATRIMOINE RURAL

TÂCHE FINALE

Vous rédigez une affichette, à l'intention de visiteurs étrangers, expliquant quels ont été l'esprit et les étapes d'un projet de restauration sur votre commune (vieille grange, moulin à eau ou à vent).

ACTIVITÉ LANGAGIÈRE	NIVEAU VISÉ
Expression écrite	**A2+**

CAPACITÉS À METTRE EN ŒUVRE

⚙ Écrire des phrases simples dans un texte articulé.

⚙ Décrire simplement et brièvement des lieux et leur histoire.

⚙ Apporter de l'information simple mais précise sur un sujet concret.

⚙ Réaliser une affichette, un panneau.

Memories of the past

BOÎTE À OUTILS

Qualifier	Adjectifs épithètes et attributs	The door looks old. The barn's got red tiles.
	Adverbes	She really looks after the roof. He is always working.
	Mots composés	It's a clear-water pond. Did you notice it was hand-made? It's really time-consuming.
Exposer/ illustrer/ donner des exemples	Outils de présentation et d'organisation du propos	Here is / There is / First / Then / Finally / It comes from / It's the result of / The point is / As a matter of fact / By the way.
		This is an offer you can't refuse. What I mean is we're pretty busy rebuilding the walls at the moment.
	L'introduction	Well, to begin with, I'd like to explain what we intend to do, exactly.
	L'analogie	Take this morning, for example: …
Démontrer/ justifier/ persuader	Articulations du discours	Because / But / For / For that reason / So / So that / In order to / Therefore. The reason is… The thing is… The watermill was closed for repairs.
	Relations logiques (cause, conséquence, but)	Thanks to / In order to / Due to / Because of / Since. Arrange things so that you finish tomorrow. Repair it quickly so it opens next month.
	Énoncés complexes	That's what I wanted to do but my partner didn't agree.

1

Rural architecture

Origin: © Pitstone Green Museum U.K.

Origin: cc by-sa M. Reeve

Origin: © J. Weber/INRA

2

400 years of History

Work is about to begin to re-thatch an historic 400-year-old farmhouse in Carmarthenshire as part of a major restoration project using local materials.

Aberdeunant has seen dramatic changes in Welsh rural life since it was built in the Middle Ages, although the house has survived remarkably intact. Today it belongs to National Trust Wales who rent it out to a young tenant family as part of a 150-acre organic farm.

The cruck-framed farmhouse is thought to have been rebuilt in the late medieval period as a hall-house, but despite being altered at some point every century since then, many of the original features have been preserved.

The re-thatch will take several months to complete and will be undertaken by a team of experts. A medieval variety of organic straw has been grown and harvested on a farm near Brecon ensuring the project uses authentic local materials.

Medieval-type straw is longer and more suitable for roofing than its modern counterparts and it is hoped the process of re-thatching will become a useful educational tool for local schools who have been invited to come and see the work being done.

"Aderdeunant farm is an island of bio-diversity in a sea of modern farming methods", said Wyn Davies, the National Trust's Assistant Area Warden for Carmarthenshire, "It's a testament of Welsh rural life".

10.11. 2007 - National Trust Wales

Origin: © Culture24, www.culture24.org.uk

3

The conservation of historic farm buildings

Introduction

It is a sad fact that relatively few historic farm buildings have a meaningful role in modern life. Many are neglected and are in a state of serious dilapidation or decay. It has been estimated that across the country at least one traditional barn each week is destroyed without trace, and often without record. [...]

An unusual granary barn in Chute on traditional staddlestones

New Uses

Finding a complementary new use for an old farm building is not easy. Imaginative adaptations, however, can sometimes be very successful. Recently the gable end of a listed timber framed barn has been adjusted to allow tall modern farm machinery to obtain access. In another case a small barn has been allocated to a nearby house for use as garaging. At Southcott, Pewsey, a thatched threshing barn is now being used for the production of organic cider. [...]

With inventiveness there are many options but only conversions that involve minimal alteration to the basic form, character and setting of listed historic buildings are likely to be successful. Proposed conversions of barns for example, to habitable accommodation are likely to be less successful than conversions to an open plan workshop/garage. In Ogbourne St George a new owner of a dilapidated barn gained permission for its conversion as an office and unheated display room for building materials – minimum intervention is always the key factor to consider.

Origin: © 2010 Wiltshire Council

4

Letheringsett Watermill

Norfolk's only flour producing watermill

The red brick mill you see today was built in 1802. Letheringsett watermill is the last remaining watermill in Norfolk to produce flour.

[...] Mike and Marion Thurlow took over the mill in 1987 and have restored the mill to working order and it is now an award winning tourist attraction.

[...] A speciality wheat, Spelt is milled here at Letheringsett. Originally introduced to Britain by the Romans, Spelt is higher in vitamin B and protein and other wheat, and most wheat sensitive people can tolerate spelt flour in their diet. Spelt flour is only one of the many different types of flour, dried fruit and nuts that can be purchased in the mill shop.

[...] Letheringsett mill holds regular working demonstrations of milling and a tour of the mill on most weekday afternoons. Mike usually conducts the tour himself and gives an informative and fascinating insight to the history of the mill and flour production.

For a more detailed history and photographs of Letheringsett watermill and other mills in Norfolk, visit Norfolk Mills website: www.norfolkmills.co.uk

Origin: © Anne Grand 2007

5

Circular thinking: round barns on US farms

6

Protecting hedgerows

We are committed to protecting hedgerows and dry stone walls – features which give beauty and character to rural landscapes and are valuable habitats for wildlife. Their patterns stitch the characteristic patchwork quilt over the countryside and they are intimately connected with our history and ancestors. We have long campaigned for better protection for hedgerows, and continue to do so.

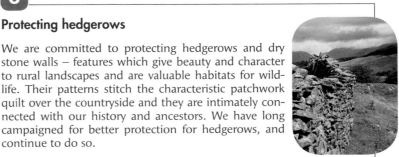

Origin: © CPRE

7

Fordson Tractor

The Fordson Model F was completed in 1916 and was the first lightweight, mass produced tractor in the world, making it possible for the average farmer to own a tractor for the first time. Ford incorporated his private company, Henry Ford and Son, Inc., to mass produce the tractor on July 27, 1917. [...] He used the same assembly line techniques he used to mass produce the Ford Model T. It took thirty hours and forty minutes to convert the raw materials into the 4,000 parts used for the tractor assembly. The Fordson sold for US$750 ($14,124 in 2007 dollars). [...]

It used a 20 horsepower, four-cylinder vaporising oil engine, a three-speed spur gear transmission (the three forward speeds ranged from approximately 2 1/4 to 6 1/4 mph). [...]

Brakes were not provided on early Fordsons [...]. To stop the tractor, the driver depressed the clutch. [...]

The Fordson succeeded in being cheaper to maintain than horses, as the Ford Model T had previously done. A government test concluded that farmers spent $.95 per acre plowing with a Fordson compared to feeding eight horses for a year and paying two drivers, which cost $1.46 per acre.

Origin: cc by-sa Wikipedia, http://en.wikipedia.org/wiki/Fordson_tractor

8

Campaign grows to save boglands

Up to fairly recent times, bogs were simply regarded as sources of fuel or useless wasteland. But attitudes have changed and nowadays bogs are looked on as being of huge environmental value, places that can tell us a great deal about our past and homes of nature.

[...] Groups such as the Irish Peatland Conservation Council (IPCC) have been campaigning to save what remains of our boglands and Bord na Móna has now committed to restoring and conserving bogs under its control. Underneath each bog is a unique combination of soil types and nutrients. These determine what a bog can be used for after its peat has been harvested. Very often, peat cannot be harvested from parts of the bog and some peaty areas are left.

Each cutaway bog requires a variety of approaches to get the best use from the land: some areas are suitable for forestry, some for grassland and some for wetland and other wildlife habitats. The mineral composition of some areas is hostile to certain plants and a haven for others. As more bogs cease production, Bord na Móna has a significant opportunity to develop land to the benefit of wildlife, the environment and communities.

[...] Thousands of men migrated from all over Ireland to work there, cutting turf for Irish homes, hospitals and businesses. Machines eventually took over the turf-cutting, but the feats of some legendary manual turf-cutters have become part of the folklore of the midland bogs.

By D. Hickey

09.07.2009

Origin: © The Irish Examiner (Cork)

9

Dorset countryside

Wake up to to Dorset countryside. Dorset looks stunning at any time of year and there is so much to do here even in the winter months. This beautiful county has so much to offer for visitors of all ages so why not stay in Dorset Farm and Country Holiday quality bed and breakfast accommodation or a self catering cottage on a farm or in the countryside.

Dorset Farm and Country Holidays offers a wide variety of high quality relaxing farmhouse bed and breakfast and self-catering holidays, mostly on working farms, in the beautiful Dorset countryside at any time of year. We offer exceptional value for money and we have no agency fees. With members across the county you have a choice of where to stay each time you return and we are all ready to give you a warm and personal welcome as you arrive. All our accommodation is regularly inspected by the Quality in Tourism Assurance scheme. [...]

Summer is not the only season to savour the delights of Dorset. It is a county for all seasons with its mild, south coast climate. The footpath network throughout the county is unsurpassed: the South West Coastal Path offers exciting scenery, with safe and sandy beaches interspersed by rugged cliffs teeming with wildlife whilst the country footpaths meander inland through hidden valleys and dramatic hills. All part of Dorset's charm.

Origin: © www.ruraldorset.co.uk

10
Bleakblow – audioguide

11
Montgomery county

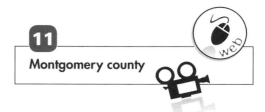

PISTES PÉDAGOGIQUES

doc. 1   Cet ensemble de photos présente des exemples de construction du patrimoine rural. On peut suggérer aux apprenants de deviner quels sont les autres éléments constitutifs de ce patrimoine : autres types de bâtiments, étangs, barrages sur rivières, ou encore machines agricoles anciennes. L'enseignant peut choisir de présenter les trois photos comme un ensemble ou d'isoler la photo de son choix, selon le niveau des apprenants et leur capacité à formuler des hypothèses.

doc. 2   Ce texte présente un exemple de sauvegarde du patrimoine. Son étude vise prioritairement à sensibiliser les apprenants aux divers buts de la sauvegarde d'un bâtiment, d'un lieu en général.

doc. 3, 4   Ces deux textes montrent des exemples de restauration de bâtiments. L'accent est mis sur la finalité économique de la sauvegarde et sur le souci de préserver le patrimoine. Pour que les apprenants saisissent clairement l'intérêt de la restauration, l'enseignant doit proposer un travail de compréhension détaillée et sélective. La classe peut être divisée en deux groupes, chacun travaillant sur un document, avec, pour tâche intermédiaire, de présenter à l'autre groupe les éléments pertinents de la compréhension sélective.

doc. 5   Ce document audio offre un contenu original. Il appartient à l'enseignant d'effectuer la didactisation de ce document, lorsqu'il a rigoureusement choisi un passage d'environ une minute à faire étudier aux apprenants. L'extrait sélectionné doit attirer l'attention sur une architecture inhabituelle.

doc. 6, 7, 8   Ces trois textes présentent d'autres facettes du patrimoine à sauvegarder. L'étude de chaque document peut être exhaustive, si elle est faite avec l'ensemble des apprenants. L'enseignant peut également proposer un travail en groupes, la restitution (orale ou écrite) constituant alors une tâche intermédiaire de communication authentique en classe.

doc. 9, 10   Le texte et le document sonore permettent d'établir le lien entre la sauvegarde du patrimoine et le tourisme rural. La densité lexicale de l'un et de l'autre nécessite une aide soutenue. Seule une fiche d'aide à la compréhension détaillée, fournie par l'enseignant (voir exemple sur le site compagnon avec les documents 10bis et 10ter), peut permettre aux apprenants d'appréhender correctement le document audio.

doc. 11   Cette vidéo apporte une ouverture supplémentaire sur le sujet. Son utilisation à des fins didactiques dépend du projet de l'enseignant. En tout état de cause la bande-son est trop complexe pour un travail de compréhension orale au niveau A2. Par contre, des sélections d'images isolées ou de séquences significatives, choisies par l'enseignant, sont de nature à stimuler la prise de parole.

TÂCHE FINALE

L'ensemble des apprenants rédige un document portant sur un chantier de restauration, l'enseignant veillant à ce que tous ne choisissent pas le même. La tâche étant écrite, un travail individuel, voire en binôme, est tout à fait adapté. Les manques, en termes d'outils linguistiques, doivent être comblés par un travail en autonomie de chaque élève, assisté par l'enseignant. Les productions écrites peuvent être mises en valeur par des photos ou des images, et faire l'objet d'un affichage en classe.

Thème 16

TOURISME RURAL

TÂCHE FINALE

Dans le cadre d'un stage à l'office de tourisme de votre ville, vous êtes chargé(e) de réaliser une affiche ou un dépliant publicitaire présentant votre région ou votre commune afin de promouvoir le tourisme local auprès de touristes étrangers.

ACTIVITÉ LANGAGIÈRE	NIVEAU VISÉ
Expression écrite	**A2**

CAPACITÉS À METTRE EN ŒUVRE

⚙ Rédiger une affiche, un dépliant.

⚙ Décrire un lieu.

⚙ Donner des conseils.

Nature never goes out of style

 BOÎTE À OUTILS

Nommer/ désigner	La détermination	This is a…
		John is the man who runs the company.
	Outils de la localisation spatiale	It's there. Where? Right here, on your left!
Caractériser /définir	Compléments du nom	The colour of the front door is amazing.
Qualifier	Adjectifs épithètes et attributs	Farnham is an old English market town.
	Adverbes	This town has always a warm welcome.
	Mots composés	It's a three-star hotel.
Situer dans l'espace	Compléments, prépositions et adverbes de lieu	On your right… / On your left…
		It's right next to/in front of the station.
		It's two miles away, you can't possibly miss it.
Donner des indications	Adverbes et locutions de temps, de lieu, de durée, de manière	When you arrive, drop in for a visit.
		Once inside, take the lift to the first floor.
Suggérer	L'expression de la suggestion	For more information go to…
	L'impératif	Don't miss the old castle.

1

Brochure

Origin: © Farm Stay UK

2

Rural and farm tourism

Although UK residents spend twice as much on countryside holidays overseas than in England, there is still a strong demand for domestic rural tourism and this demand is expected to continue to grow due to several factors. Firstly, there is an increasing interest in, and awareness of, the countryside, environment and conservation. [...]

The countryside is seen as having a diversity of landscape, culture and facilities that contrasts with the increasing standardisation of urban areas. The countryside is also perceived to be less at risk from terrorism and pollution than other types of destinations.

People are becoming more concerned about health and fitness as well and walking and cycling have become popular hobbies. The ageing population is more active than ever and seeking healthy activities like walking, cycling and exploring. [...]

There is also a growing trend of taking multiple short breaks and additional holidays, which will positively affect the future of rural tourism.

By England Research, 28th July 2005.

Origin: © VisitBritain 2004

3

Rustic tourism

Origin: © www.CartoonStock.com

4

Rough and tough: Jeff's trip to Newfoundland

5

Ecotourism

Nature never goes out of style

Why rural tourism is no picnic

There have been cows on Colemans Farm for 450 years, but these days they're just for show.

Even on a drenched autumn day, the farm is one of the Isle of Wight's perkier tourist attractions: flocks of squealing schoolchildren make friends with bleating goats and clucking chickens.

When Neil and Karen Dickson bought Colemans in 1999, it was a working farm. But it had a licence to open to the public, and the island location persuaded the Dicksons that it could make more money farming tourists.

And so it proved. On their first day, the Dicksons had 600 visitors; last year, they had 60,000, and growth rates have been 30-40 % annually. The farm is now profitable, and the Dicksons are planning a big expansion next year. [...]

Now, tourism supports 380,000 jobs in rural areas, more than making up for a decline of more than 150,000 in the agricultural workforce. Overall, its contribution to rural economic output is reckoned to be almost £14bn.

The lure of easy money is strong. But Nick Evans, who runs the Centre for Rural Research at University College Worcester, warns that tourism is no panacea for every cash-strapped farmer.

For a start, he says, the realistic profit to be made from a tourism sideline is little better than pin-money. [...]

Nonetheless, there are certain unarguable fundamental benefits.

If expectations of income are low, tourism can be run as a complementary sideline. Farms tend to have plentiful barely-used space, ripe for conversion; a B&B or holiday cottage can be run by a less busy family member. [...]

And tourism may be vaguely seasonal, but often in ways that suit a farmer's schedule: the peak for many tourist businesses would be in high summer, before the demands of the harvest kick in. [...]

Despite its growth, tourism makes up just 9 % of rural employment; manufacturing, meanwhile, employs one in four rural workers, and is growing at a fair clip.

J. Arnold

Origin: © from BBC News at bbc.co.uk/news

7

The return of the hippies

Some people just go on holiday. Other go backpacking. But those who are really eco-conscious go "wwoofing". Most of us may think "wwoofing" is something only dogs do.

In fact, it is a huge, international movement that allows people to travel to almost any country, live for free, become friends with the locals and make cheese. Or wine. Or even sake.

WWOOF (World-Wide Opportunities on Organic Farms) is an organization that started in Britain in 1971, at the height of the hippy era. It is generally imagined that the hippy dream ended in a haze of drugs and lost idealism. Not true. Even if most of the world embraced rampant capitalism, 4x4 cars, and credit cards, a determined few remained true to the ideals of the movement and are still successfully living the hippy lifestyle. The idealism of those in the WWOOF movement, in particular, is still intact.

The idea of wwoofing is simple: you travel to another country, but instead of staying in hotels, you live and work on organic farms, working a couple of hours each day in return for food, a bed, and warm hospitality. No money changes hands, and those who have tried wwoofing find the experience more enriching than being an ordinary tourist.

"I have stayed with about seven hosts throughout Japan and really enjoyed every one of them", says an Australian wwoofer. "Each experience was so different, and we met such a variety of people, that I feel like I am returning to Australia with so many new ideas how to live life, and have friends and family in Japan forever".

The beauty of wwoofing is that it allows people to travel for much longer than they would as an ordinary tourist because all they need to do is get from one place to the next. And even that need not cost money. Thomas and Katja are a German couple who spent a whole year bicycling around New Zealand. They stayed at no less than 26 different farms and cooperatives, yet they had ample time to explore the country along the way: "Apart from cycling and wwoofing, we explored the country by foot and with kayaks, climbed mountains and walked many tracks. We melted snow for water, washed in Crystal rivers, and soaked in hot thermal pools. We spent a year in nature".

Origin: © Bayard Presse/*Today in English,* April 2008

8

Matt talks about wwoofing

9

Wwoofing: Is it for you?

Why Do It

- Healthy lifestyle – you'll eat fresh organic food and get your workout.
- City dwellers might find the peace of mind they needed to de-stress.
- You can work on your language skills if you choose a farm abroad.
- Being in a different environment can greatly help creativity.
- You might spend a lot of time alone.

Why Not Do It

- You might spend a lot of time alone (too much of one thing can be bad).
- You might have to pay a membership fee so you can provide free labor for someone.
- Internet might not be available or it might be slow or limited.
- You might share a room with several people, which might be especially uncomfortable if there are personality clashes.
- You might be too tired to get much freelancing work done.
- Working on a farm is unpredictable and you might be asked to work longer than what you'd agreed on.

A. da Silva

Origin: http://freelanceswitch.com/blog/

10

Farnham leaflet

Welcome To Farnham

Getting to Farnham

Farnham is at the meeting point of several main roads and is easy to reach by public and private transport. It is within an hour's drive of Heathrow and Gatwick, is linked to London Waterloo by rail and is connected to other centres via bus.

Farnham will surprise you!

Just an hour's drive from London, on modern high speed roads, take the turning and you enter a different world. Farnham is an old English market town with narrow streets lined with some of the finest Georgian architecture in the South of England with a parish church and castle dating back to the 12th Century. Farnham has a host of attractions for visitors, and its historic character combines with the best of modern facilities.

With a wealth of tempting opportunities for escaping to the countryside, shopping, eating out, sightseeing, visiting galleries or just sitting in gardens and flower filled yards soaking up the enchanting atmosphere. Farnham always has a warm welcome for visitors.

NORTH DOWNS WAY NATIONAL TRAIL DOVER 153 MILES

Farnham Town

Farnham is a vibrant and lively country market town with its own elegant style and a depth of character derived from many centuries of history. Farnham town offers a unique experience with its traditional shopping high street, its award winning museum and the fact that it's a creative town with several excellent galleries, a craft study centre, the Farnham Maltings and much more...

For more information:
Email: tourism@farnham.gov.uk
Tel: 01252 712667
Web: www.farnham.gov.uk
Farnham Town Council Office, South Street
Farnham, Surrey GU9 7RN

Origin: © Farnham Town Council

PISTES PÉDAGOGIQUES

doc. 1   Cette couverture de dépliant touristique introduit le thème du tourisme rural. Les apprenants sont amenés, en décrivant le document, à réfléchir sur la notion de tourisme rural.

doc. 2   Ce texte fournit des explications sur les raisons du succès du tourisme rural. Avant de découvrir le texte dans son intégralité, l'enseignant peut choisir, dans un premier temps, de ne faire lire que la première phrase et demander aux apprenants d'émettre des hypothèses sur les raisons de ce succès. La lecture du texte en entier doit permettre de vérifier la liste des hypothèses des apprenants, et de la compléter le cas échéant.

doc. 3   Ce document iconographique souligne le paradoxe des adeptes du tourisme rural. Il permet de réutiliser le lexique vu au travers des documents précédents et de revoir les notions permettant d'exprimer le conseil ou le reproche.

doc. 4   Ce document audio propose une discussion entre deux anglophones sur des vacances à Terre-Neuve. Il peut être l'occasion d'un travail sur le champ lexical du tourisme et du voyage, et notamment sur les adjectifs liés à la notion de ruralité.

doc. 5   Ce document audio définit la notion d'écotourisme. Il doit, en raison de sa longueur, être exploité en deux temps. La première partie (jusqu'à «*would you prefer something different?*») présente une vision des vacances idéales, sur laquelle les apprenants sont amenés à réfléchir («Est-ce votre conception des vacances? Existe-t-il des alternatives?»). Les apprenants peuvent remplir un tableau dans lequel ils déterminent les caractéristiques de chaque conception du tourisme. La comparaison des deux visions apporte des arguments aux apprenants pour leur permettre de prendre position.

doc. 6   Cet article traite de l'évolution du tourisme rural, et plus particulièrement de l'ouverture des exploitations agricoles aux touristes, les «fermes touristiques» étant en constante augmentation au Royaume-Uni. Les apprenants doivent relever les raisons de cette évolution, ainsi que les avantages et les risques que cela comporte pour les exploitants et les touristes.

doc. 7, 8   Ce texte et ce document audio traitent du phénomène du *wwoofing* (*World-Wide Opportunities on Organic Farming*), une autre alternative au tourisme rural classique. Le document 7 est un article qui définit ce mode de tourisme en le comparant au mouvement hippie des années 60. Le document audio 8 est le témoignage d'un jeune Canadien sur son expérience de *wwoofer*. À partir de ces deux documents, les apprenants peuvent compléter le tableau réalisé précédemment, lors de l'étude du document 5.

doc. 9   Ce texte présente des arguments contraires sur le *wwoofing*. Il permet de travailler l'expression de la modalité (*might, may, should*).

doc. 10   À partir de cet extrait d'un dépliant touristique, l'enseignant peut amener les apprenants à réfléchir sur la construction du document et les informations essentielles qu'il contient. Les apprenants peuvent s'inspirer de ce document pour réaliser la tâche finale.

TÂCHE FINALE

Pour réaliser une affiche ou un dépliant présentant leur région, les apprenants sont invités à rechercher, sur Internet ou à l'office de tourisme, des informations précises sur, par exemple, l'hébergement, les transports (l'accès), les atouts (culturels, climatiques) de la région.
Ils rédigent des textes courts qu'ils illustrent par des photos ou des plans.

Crédits

Nous tenons à remercier vivement toutes les personnes et les organismes qui nous ont accordé les droits de reproduction à titre gracieux. Les crédits des documents iconographiques, des documents audio et des documents vidéo sont indiqués par thème avec le numéro du document correspondant.

Domaine 1 : © M. Meuret/INRA

Thème 1 – Photo d'illustration du thème : cc by-sa R. McKee
Doc. 5 : © Helppuppies.com/PETA
Doc. 10 : © 2010 Knowlera Media LLC

Thème 2 – Photo d'illustration du thème : © C. Maitre/INRA
Doc. 3 : cc by T. Pierce
Doc. 4 : manipulation génétique : © J. Weber/INRA
Brin d'ADN : © S. Dusko Ehrlich/INRA
Doc. 7 : © Arcadia Biosciences
Doc. 8 : cc by AZRainmann
Doc. 10 : © Abby Martin

Thème 3 – Photo d'illustration du thème : © J. Weber/INRA
Doc. 6 : © P. Boudias
Doc. 11 : © P. Boudias

Thème 4 – Photo d'illustration du thème : © F. Brioudes/INRA
Doc. 2 : poulet : cc by-sa W. Merydith
Eggmobile : cc by-sa M. Burks
Doc. 6 : © VOA Special English
Doc. 9 : © VOA Special English
Doc. 11 : © Bonnie Lee Bucqueroux

Domaine 2 : © V. Desjardins

Thème 5 – Photo d'illustration du thème : © R. Burbaud
Doc. 5 : © Farming & Countryside Education
Doc. 7 : © VOA Special English
Doc. 8 : © George Jackman
Doc. 11 : © Plumpton College, Business in Vision 2009

Thème 6 – Photo d'illustration du thème : © R. Canta/INRA
Doc. 8 : J. Leech, *Mr. Briggs, Pleasures of Hunting*, in *Punch magazine*, 1850

Thème 7 – Photo d'illustration du thème : © Smithsonian Institution
Doc. 5 : © P. Boudias
Doc. 6 : © P. Boudias
Doc. 7 : © P. Boudias
Doc. 8 : © 2006-2010 VideoJug Corporation Limited
Doc. 9 : cc by J. Okada
Doc. 10 : © P. Boudias
Doc. 12 : cc by M. Buck
Doc. 13 : © VOA Special English

Thème 8 – Photo d'illustration du thème : © R. Burbaud
Doc. 3 : © VOA Special English
Doc. 11 : This material was provided courtesy of U.S. National Park Service. Additional information about U.S. national parks can be found at http://www.nps.gov

Domaine 3 : cc by G. Maclean

Thème 9 – Photo d'illustration du thème : © R. Burbaud
Doc. 4 : © Secretariat of the Convention on Biological Diversity, http://www.cbd.int/secretariat/
Doc. 7 : © Secretariat of the Convention on Biological Diversity, http://www.cbd.int/secretariat/
Doc. 9 : © Secretariat of the Convention on Biological Diversity, http://www.cbd.int/secretariat/
Doc. 10 : These materials first appeared at www.britishcouncil.org/learnenglish and are used with the permission of the British Council

Thème 10 – Photo d'illustration du thème : © R. Burbaud
Doc. 7 : © CAST, http://cast-science.org
Doc. 11 : © 2006 Frederick Deligne, Nice-Matin, France, and PoliticalCartoons.com
Doc. 12 : © Todd Beuckens
Doc. 13 : © Todd Beuckens

Thème 11 – Photo d'illustration du thème : © R. Burbaud
Doc. 3 : © European Union, 2010
Doc. 7 : © Todd Beuckens
Doc. 11 : These materials first appeared at www.britishcouncil.org/learnenglish and are used with the permission of the British Council
Doc. 13 : © University of Warwick

Thème 12 – Photo d'illustration du thème : © Smithsonian Institution
Doc. 2 : cc by Y. Ono
Doc. 3 : cc by M. Malz
Doc. 6 : © VOA Special English
Doc. 8 : © FAO/Giuseppe Bizzarri
Doc. 9 : plante vase : cc by-sa K. Teague
Eau bouillonnante et plante : cc by-sa P. Semanaz
Doc. 10 : © J.-M. Bossennec/INRA
Doc. 12 : © Greenpeace International, www.greenpeace.org

Domaine 4 : © AlcelVision

Thème 13 – Photo d'illustration du thème : © F. Carreras/INRA
Doc. 3 : vente sur le marché : © 2 Sisters Farm Fresh Eggs & Vegetables
Banderole : © Experimental Station
Doc. 7 : © 2011 Slow Food
Doc. 8 : cc by-sa Christine H.
Doc. 9 : © VOA Special English

Thème 14 – Photo d'illustration du thème : © Dave_S
Doc. 3 : © CAPOC
Doc. 4 : © RIP Save our rural communities
Doc. 6 : © The Comission For Rural Communities and Manches Research
Doc. 10 : post&go et post office: cc by-sa sludgegulper/Felix O

Thème 15 – Photo d'illustration du thème : © Steve Hodgson
Doc. 4 : Watermill et roue à aube : cc by-sa S. & J. Copley
Doc. 5 : © VOA Special English
Doc. 6 : cc by J. Goulden
Doc. 7 : © Library of Congress
Doc. 8 : cc by Lews Castle UHI, www.uhi.ac.uk/ruralstudies/
Doc. 10 : © Moors for the Future Partnership
Doc. 11 : © 2005 Heritage Montgomery

Thème 16 – Photo d'illustration du thème : © R. Burbaud
Doc. 4 : © Todd Beuckens
Doc. 5 : These materials first appeared at www.britishcouncil.org/learnenglish and are used with the permission of the British Council
Doc. 8 : © Studio TDES, www.thedailyenglishshow.com
Doc. 10 : © D. Azan

Nous avons fait tout notre possible pour établir l'identité de tous les détenteurs des droits et l'éditeur est disposé à rectifier les éventuelles erreurs ou omissions dans les futures rééditions. Les droits de ces détenteurs leur restent réservés.